The Deceit of Rome

The Roman Catholic Church, an invented institution
based on lies, intrigues and malpractice

Maurits Prins

Published by:
Trine Day LLC
PO Box 577
Walterville, OR 97489
1-800-556-2012
www.TrineDay.com
trineday@icloud.com

Library of Congress Control Number: 2019931691

Prins, Maurits
 – 1st ed.
p. cm.
Includes references
Epub (ISBN-13) 978-1-63424-235-6
Mobi (ISBN-13) 978-1-63424-236-3
Print (ISBN-13) 978-1-63424-234-9
1. RELIGION -- Christianity -- History. 2. Catholic Church -- Controversial lit-erature. . 3. Christianity -- Origin. 4. Jesus Christ -- Family. 5. France -- Rennes-le-Château. 6. Gnosticism. 7. Apocryphal Gospels. I. Prins, Maurits II. Title

First Edition
10 9 8 7 6 5 4 3 2 1

Printed in the USA

Distribution to the Trade by:
Independent Publishers Group (IPG)
814 North Franklin Street
Chicago, Illinois 60610
312.337.0747
www.ipgbook.com

In the beginning was the Word, and the Word was with God, and the Word was God. He was with God in the beginning. Through him all things were made; without him nothing was made that has been made. In him was life, and that life was the light of all mankind. The light shines in the darkness, and the darkness has not overcome it.

CONTENTS

FOREWORD

A s the author of this book, I agree with the issues presented by Nelson Mandela, the former president of South Africa, who died not so long ago. He devoted his endeavors to connection and reconciliation, but first, to reach this state of enlightenment, he had to go through a very personal process. I too have learned to consider carefully my position in life and to convert some of my disadvantages into advantages. I realized I could only achieve that by being open to insights from others and reflecting within myself.

Self-reflection, meditation, and most of all acceptance, were the necessary themes for me. An important part of this process was facing my own ego, an issue that necessarily had to be addressed. I discovered that my ego had become so dominant, that this was an obstacle on my way to higher consciousness. Thereby the focus was on the events of my past, and in my future ideals and expectations. This is our common cultural inheritance. It keeps us from living in the *now* and focusing on the things that really matter. In my work as a therapist, it was a matter of course for me to be silent and empty my head, in order to gain insight into the problems of my clients.

I mention this, because I want to be pure and transparent about my reasons for writing this book, for I can imagine that you as a reader will experience it as an accusation against the Catholic Church.

This, however, is not the main purpose. I want to clarify the foundations of Christianity, that has its origin in the Roman Catholic Church. In addition, for the followers of conservatism in the Church, which is characterized by a certain degree of narcissism, I want to show that it does not make sense to stick to something that is not true.

I know that among the current generations of dignitaries and priests within the Catholic Church are honest men, working servants, a few of whom I know personally. Of course, there have been sincere people within the Church throughout the centuries. I know many priests have a clear vision with a realistic view on humanity.

This book has become my personal digestion process of all the traumas that I have accumulated during many lives through the ages. However, the same goes for everyone because to me, it is an established fact that a human being has several lives. I found proof of this, in regression therapy. I discovered that many traumas originate from past lives and often have to do with having been burned and tortured, for instance during the period of the Inquisition.

From more than forty years of practice, I have created the circumstances in which many of these traumas can be digested.

My own process has been completed. The feelings of anger and fear have been replaced by reconciliation and forgiveness. Thereby, during a session, after processing their trauma, I taught also to others how to convert everything into Love and Light.

Then of course, the question arises: who and what should I forgive? Especially when looking from a bigger perspective on life. For I am convinced that the Catholic Church and everything that originated from it, has had its purpose. In my opinion, everything is necessary and in the end, nothing is wasted for it helps us to grow and evolve.

Forgiveness is something one usually gives directly to a person or a group, but I offer my forgiveness to the Church as a whole. To reconcile oneself with the other and to forgive them is liberating. I can say this from my own personal experience.

Many readers will identify with this book, which at the same time has a therapeutic effect.

In addition, I invite church leaders to look at their true story with an open mind and self- reflection. In my opinion, they can do so without any reserve. Stop defending what no longer can be defended! Nobody will lose, not even the current theologians, for honesty and good will are always justifiable.

This does not change the positive effect the Church has. The Church will also not stop existing. On the contrary, the Church will undergo a change and will be able to contribute to humanity's growth of consciousness.

Moreover, the consequence of that change is that, only then, is real redemption possible for a large part of humanity.

Pope Francis has already started renewal and shows us that even a man holding an important position can be humble, which has a huge effect. He is a good example for us all.

INTRODUCTION

As a child, I grew up in a traditional Catholic family in the southern Netherlands. My faith, like that of many others, originated in my upbringing. Anything the Church taught as the truth was what people were thinking in general.

I cherished the ceremonies and rituals. The atmosphere caused by candle-light, the scent of incense, the songs and the music, created an ambience that really appealed to me.

However, even at my young age, I felt that something was not right. I could not find the words to explain what it was that held me back. Besides that, a dilemma presented itself: On the one hand, my parents taught me to be loyal to the Roman Catholic Church and on the other hand, they told me to always be honest and stay critical.

That was all I knew, for my mother was a very critical person. She did not always agree with the statements of the Church. I remember still her habit on Sunday, after the Holy Mass, of taking a closer look at the sermon.

When I look at this now, I can understand it very well, because she always combined her religious experience with her intuitive inner life. Because of this, her attitude was different from others and she noticed that some elements of the Church's dogma were not consistent with her personal experience.

When she was talking to priests, she also had no reserve in defending her views. She could be quite sharp to the officiating priest or chaplain. I remember the occasion when a chaplain visited our home, to inquire when the family would expect the next child. I can still hear her words of anger. "What are you thinking? It is none of your business! If this is what you came for, you'd better leave right now!" Now, many years later, I can fully confirm this; for I share her experience that much of what the Church wants believers to believe without question is completely opposite to what I personally experience. To give an example: The Church teaches that the soul, after death, moves to heaven, purgatory or hell, depending on how a person has lived. However, when as a child, I told my mother I had seen my grandfather, she explained that what I saw and experienced was a proof of life on the other side. My grandfather was not at all in heaven or in hell, in fact he was suddenly standing in my bedroom. I was taken by surprise, although I was used to seeing people who passed away. I was shocked too, because this was my own grandfather and that changed the experience. It is not the same as if I saw someone I did not know. I pinched my arm to check if I was awake. I was not dreaming, for sure! When my grandfather noticed that I was convinced of what I had seen, he disappeared again.

This sort of occurrence regularly happened at my home. One morning, my mother said to my father, "Today, Ferdinand Miras is going to pay us a visit!" My dad initially had to laugh. In his view, this was impossible, for they had not heard from this man for more than twenty years. Nevertheless, he was not completely sure, because he knew very well that his wife, having premonitions like this, was usually proven right. That same day, around noon, Ferdinand stood in front of the door.

Following the common practice in my time and environment, I became an acolyte and chorister. Without thinking, I did what I was expected to do, but what surprised me, was the general attitude within the Church towards liturgical objects. We were not allowed to touch a chalice, ciborium or monstrance with our bare hands. Only the priest was allowed to do so, because his hands were consecrated. If we touched one of these items anyway, we knew something bad would happen to us. Aside from that, it was a sin and you had to confess a sin. If we did not do so, we would go to hell. We were bound to get into trouble. On many occasions, I thought to myself, "This is such nonsense!" One day, despite many warnings, I mustered all my courage. At a certain time, when nobody was around in the consistory, I took the chalice in my hands. At first, I felt hesitant, but when I noticed nothing out of the ordinary happened, I took hold of this sacred object and, in a feeling of triumph, convinced myself nothing was happening. To this day, I have not succumbed to a chronic disease because of my sacrilege.

My parents were very pious people, but they were aware of the fact that, even in the Church, everything was a work of man. For that reason, they always listened to their own inner voice first.

For example, my parents taught me that there was no need to accept certain forms of physical contact or intimacy, not even from priests or monks. I remember an incident from primary school. Monks ran the school I attended, in The Hague. The teacher of the 6th grade was a small fat monk, a clingy kind of man. In those days, the teacher would sit behind a big lectern, placed on a platform. One day, he asked me to come to the front. He went over my homework, while I stood beside his chair. Suddenly, I felt his hand slide over my leg. First, it went down and then up again. He tried to slip his fingers underneath the leg of my shorts. My parents' lesson shot through my mind. I stretched my arm out and slapped him on the shoulder. He probably had not expected a thirteen-year-old boy to act like that. Nevertheless, I was successful! The teacher immediately stopped and his face went scarlet. I raced back to my spot and he never attempted it again.

It is understandable that this kind of misconduct stems from personal frustration. Unfortunately, there were, and still are, many instances of child abuse never brought out into the open. If something happened that became public, it was quickly covered up again. Although this kind of abuse has gotten more publicity in the past decade, most of it is still covered up carefully. Therefore, I find it hard to avoid the impression that the leaders of the Church will always do their utmost to preserve their public image. I know that I am not the only one who feels this way.

When I was seventeen, I entered a monastery that belonged to a congregation of friars. The peace and silence I found there appealed to me. The fact that my older brother was a member of the same congregation probably played a part in this. The congregation occupied itself with education and caring for psychiatric patients. The home I lived in at the time was connected to a boarding school for boys. Aside from education, a lot of attention was given to sports, study and recreation. I remember very well, that there were brothers who experienced personal problems dealing with sexual issues and who had affectionate bonds with some boys. I do not wish to be the judge of that. These bonds were euphemized as "special friendships" and forbidden by the rules of the monastery. The celibacy of monks and priests is a regulation that goes against human nature, causing the person to grow crooked and to possibly associate with children placed in their care, in an unacceptable way.

My activities were predominantly in the monastery itself and therefore I was not involved with the boarding school. During those days, I was taken up with studying and my passion for music. Shortly before I turned 22, I resigned. I was facing the choice of taking "the eternal vow," but I knew I could not make a lifelong connection to a way of life that I could not fully support. The procedure that followed my decision says a lot about the power of the Church. In order to resign, I had to ask permission of the Holy See (Holy Chair), the official name for the Vatican. I got frustrated, because they kept me waiting for two months and I was eager to start a new life. They informed me that I could not discuss this with anybody, not even after receiving Rome's permission to go. One night, they told me to get ready to leave early next morning. Leaving meant somebody took me to another congregation home, where nobody knew me. I had to stay there for another week. The whole process was very mysterious and secretive. After that week, I received a one-hour notice that I was to prepare myself for leaving once more. Somebody took me to a monastery in Venray, where I received a set of new clothes and some pocket money. Then, somebody took me to Nijmegen and put me on the train to The Hague, where my parents lived.

As an adolescent, developing into an adult, I came across some situations that I thankfully have distanced. From my own experience, however, I know what is happening behind the scenes. They keep up outward appearances of a celibate life, when the reality is completely different. Fortunately, it was not like this everywhere. Without doubt, there have always been clergymen who live their lives in purity.

Shortly after my return from the monastery, I met someone of my own age, who had left a different order a little while ago. Both of us had not partaken in society between the ages of 17 and 22, and that meant we missed an important part of our development. Bert and I made a step-by-step plan, in order to re-adapt ourselves to a normal life. To give an example, we still tended to walk with our hands in our sleeves. It was early 1958. We learned to dance and were terribly shy. When we tried to ask a girl to dance, we turned scarlet. We wanted to get rid of these sorts of peculiarities as soon as possible, and it worked, for within a year nobody would have guessed that we had once been monks. Our success originated from the fact, that we did not avoid any circumstances. On top of that, we kept encouraging one another.

Within myself, I always experienced a desire to be of service to others. During this period, the idea became stronger to make a living out of it. I made a list of my skills and decided to stay with psychology, because I had been studying this during my monastic period. Apart from that, I took courses in a medical as well as a psychiatric hospital.

During the sixties, while studying, I got in touch with psychic researcher Professor William Tenhaeff. At a meeting, I met Gerard Croiset, a very well-known clairvoyant. That was the moment I found out that what I saw and felt is reserved for only a few.

As a child, I could talk to my parents about all of my experiences and insights. Their view was that what I experienced was normal. After all, my mother experienced the same sort of things. I started to realize that I was talented in this field and I felt grateful.

Following Croiset's advice, I started to put my talents to use. People came to me for advice and I used my clairvoyant capabilities to help them in many fields. The results were very encouraging. Gradually it turned into a practice, in which I was active as a psychic as well as a psychosocial therapist.

During my work, I encountered much sadness and misery. My clients dealt with big emotional issues. Blockades, in the emotional life of women, were a recurring theme.

The most striking fact of all was that even monks and nuns came to me. I remember a woman who told me she had been a nun. In her dreams, she was continuously chased by a monk who wanted to rape her. Usually, while conducting a conversation, I spontaneously receive clairvoyant images from the person. In this case, I was taken back to a period in which women were prosecuted and condemned as witches. I saw a monk, clad in a black and white habit, who accused her of seducing him. I discovered there are women who have carried experiences like this along with them through several lives.

I also met a pastor who was still active in his parish and felt weighed down by a huge moral dilemma. On the one hand, he functioned as a priest, and on the other hand, he was in a relationship with a woman he loved. Following my advice, he finally resigned his office in the church and half a year later he found employment as a teacher in a secondary school. When I saw him again, he told me a burden had been lifted from his shoulders.

I remember a nun visited my practice, who was dealing with emotional problems because the nuns within her community bullied and neglected her. She lived in a small monastery and was the one who dealt with all the household chores. The co-sisters looked down upon this nun, because they themselves worked in the field of education. In order to be able to help her, I had to contact her mother superior. The provincial superior also lived in the same monastery. The three of them came to my practice a week later. It was a completely new experience for me to be a mediator, but in my own way, I managed to convince both superiors that they had to take measures to solve the problems and had to do so in a loving way. Monasteries are simply communities of people who can fall victim to domination and manipulation.

Despite the fact that my practice was very busy, I maintained a keen interest in the background of the Christian religion. Ever since my childhood years, I wanted to find out how it started and what had gone wrong. I studied the Bible and the apocryphal writings. I read books by cultural historians and other researchers. This last century, much has been published about the development of the Church and I collected all kinds of materials for study.

While reading these books, I would spontaneously receive clairvoyant images of events that had taken place in several ages. People have always been treated atrociously. The images I received were horrible. For instance, I was shown how people were tortured during the time of the Inquisition, for the simple reason that they had a mind of their own. My dreams, too, revealed a lot to me and sometimes I was even carried away in a vision. In one of those visions, I saw an inquisitor take a woman from a dungeon and then rape her. Then he accused her of seducing him, after which they killed the woman immediately.

I was looking for confirmation and so I asked a fellow regression therapist, if he could do some sessions with me. During these five sessions, it became clear to me that I had been active in several strategic positions within the Roman Catholic Church. I also discovered that I had undergone tremendous suffering during the persecutions in the early ages of Christianity. After these sessions, I harbored a deep aversion to visiting Rome, a subject that really occupied my mind. From the depths of my subconscious, many things came to the surface. I found the confirmation I had been looking for, but I also received lots of valuable complementary information. Among other things, I found out that I myself had been a Cardinal and even an inquisitor.

In 2002, I visited Rome. The visit was not self-evident; it was preceded by some occurrences. I had built up an attitude of resistance towards everything that had to do with the Catholic Church and so I obviously never intended to go to Rome. During that year, my family and I spent a holiday in Tuscany, Italy. An incredibly beautiful region. However, the most special thing about it was that during this stay in Tuscany, I gave up my long-time resistance to pay a visit to Rome. One morning at breakfast, I told my wife and children that I intended to go to Rome the next day. They looked at me in amazement and were very quiet. After a little while, my oldest son reacted, "Are you okay, daddy?" Very understandable from his point of view because I had never hidden the fact that in my view only a complete idiot would consider visiting Rome. I must admit, that it was beyond my comprehension; I simply woke up with the feeling that I had to go. The only thing I knew at that moment was that I'd had a dream, but I did not recall where the dream had occurred. The need to visit Rome was so strong, that I managed to convince my family. During this visit, I experienced many contradictory emotions and it felt like I was turned upside down. Experiencing Rome had not taken away my feelings of resistance against the Church. On the contrary, these feelings were strengthened further by everything that I came across there. My resistance was growing, and I felt more assertive. Some sort of alarm had gone off. It was clear that I could no longer avoid the issue and I realized that I had to deal with it one way or another.

Upon my return to our holiday home, I struggled. Rome had created quite a stir inside me and I wondered how I should deal with it.

That night, I had a dream in which I was walking around in Rome. There was a medieval monastery, or an old castle, and I saw a spiral staircase going down. I went down that staircase and entered a cellar in which no light could penetrate. In the darkness I felt my way, touching the wall, and found a candleholder made of iron that still held a piece of candle. I searched my pocket, found a box of matches and lit the candle. By the light of the candle, I could see niches that were closed off by iron fences. From one of these niches came a sound of moaning. I took the candle and followed the sound. In the niche, I saw a man, lying on the floor. He turned his face toward the light and looked at me. I could discern a reddish beard. In his eyes, I could see that he was begging me to get him out of there.

I tried to open the fence by pulling it forcefully, but it did not give way. I now recall that I was not at all afraid. Straw covered the floor and the smell was horrible. When I held the candle between the bars of the fence, I could see that the man was chained to a short beam. The beam in its turn was chained to the wall. Suddenly, I nearly jumped out of my skin when I saw a rat scurrying about. I was so shocked that I dropped the candle, which caused the straw to catch fire. I ran as fast as I could up the stairs again. I was very confused when a man approached me, bearing the same face I had seen in the dungeon. After this, I woke up.

The meaning of this dream was clear to me; I myself was the man in the dungeon because a state of not wanting to go to Rome captured me. That is why I had to go to Rome: to liberate myself.

Looking back, I can say that I am very glad this happened at that time, because upon my return it made my search for the truth even more intense.

During my first visit to Rennes-le-Château, I happened to come in touch with the spirit of a deceased person who was connected to this place. During the very special encounter the "spirit" showed me that the Catholic Church is insincere and has always kept many things hidden.

In several conversations, I noticed that I am not the only one who perceives the Church in a negative light. I heard more evidence of this than I had previously known.

I felt the need to share my experiences on paper, and the need kept growing stronger. There was, however, also fear, and it grew stronger during the writing process. I feared the consequences of writing down all I knew. Despite the fact that others told me this made no sense, and being aware of the fact that, nowadays, there is a separation between Church and state, the fear of being persecuted was giving me strong doubts.

When I was in the church of Rennes-le-Château, the long dead Bérenger Saunière himself requested me to write this book, and I could no longer resist it. He showed himself to me in a flash and I heard his voice: a very special experience that will stick in my mind forever.

Despite my initial fears, I decided to follow through. It is my intent to present a clear image of the degree to which Christian history is in disarray. It took another few years before I could put this fear into perspective and let go. Looking at it from the present, my life has been a quest, as well as a process of dealing with several other earlier lives.

Nowadays, we are witnesses of how the Christian churches attract fewer and fewer people and how spirituality is taking its place within society at the same time. Spirituality and consciousness are growing. More and more people experience an inner growth, and this makes the subconscious open up, which brings inner knowing to the surface. The spiritual value has developed from Gnosticism. "Gnosis" is about inner knowledge, a knowing that people in ancient times could rely on, because in those days people followed their intuition and the thinking mind was considered inferior. Nowadays our spirituality follows the same rules. Our talents are hidden within our intuitive life. Thankfully, more and more people experience a spiritual growth.

I am not the only one to question a number of things, because the true aspect of the Church has been criticized before.

Driven by my curiosity I researched several Christian sects, like the Lutherans, the Baptists, the Pentecostal Church and some Evangelical movements. I participated in their ceremonies and started some fierce debates.

These debates often focused on Bible texts. My interpretation of those differed completely from theirs. Some texts contradict themselves, in my view.

I encountered the same themes everywhere: *power, ego* and *fear*. It became clear to me that in all Christian factions Bible texts were interpreted in different ways, not all of them commendable. As an example: when somebody showed criticism and pointed out some weak areas and persisted, they often referred to "the angel of light," from a Bible text dealing with the devil. This happened to me also, and I left with the feeling of having been cast out. There was also frequent reference to "the lost one," and this term would be applied to both those who are not Christian and those who are Christian but do not belong to their circle. This way of thinking is hypocritical, and I encountered it within all Christian religious communities.

On the one hand, they encourage people, but on the other hand, they spin texts to give themselves a higher status and to vent their frustrations on their fellow believers.

I also encountered a religious community that focused on concordant translations. Their translations are straight from the Greek and they try to show the literal meaning. They discovered that many words have been given the wrong meaning. However, even they do not realize that the Bible is an assembled book that presents a distorted image and that men made up most of it to suit their own interests.

During the1970's, the number of churchgoing people fell into a steep decline and many turned their backs on religion. The former churchgoers now discovered themselves and started to develop their personal freedom. Many people discovered a new spiritual perspective and became conscious of their own inner strength. Spirituality started to blossom and now, in this day and age, one can no longer neglect it.

Currently, many ages-old veils are falling away and more and more things come out into the open. Evidence is presented of priests, bishops and other dignitaries to be guilty of pedophilia. The Roman institution has preserved these wrongdoings by systematically hiding them from the outside world.

Personally, I am convinced that sexual abuse has alwys been present and only increased ever since they institutionalized celibacy. During the time when Church and State were not separated, there was always a massive lack of personal freedom. Until the 1950's and 60's, even talking publicly about sex was a kind of heresy.

From my point of view, this institution was the cause of a titanic human tragedy, which was not immediately visible and therefore was not recognized. Vatican City is an internationally-acknowledged independent State, and because of that one could cover up almost anything.

I realize that this book's contents do not correspond in any way with the theological teachings the Christian churches disseminate.

In my view, the official church teachings are false, as I discovered that the writings of the New Testament are no more than a limited selection from thousands of fragments. The chosen texts were manipulated and regularly revised. They added or omitted all kinds of information. As we know them, the biblical gospels are falsified and hold many gaps.

Thanks to the endless manipulation and indoctrination of the Church, many people (especially the poorly educated) are still quite gullible and follow the myths without further thought. To be clear, a myth is a hypothetical story, which is adopted in the tradition as a metaphorical truth.

Thinking realistically about infallibility and dogma, it is only natural to conclude that this is unacceptable. Even a pope, just like any other human being, is imperfect and transitory.

I do not merely want to attack the institution of the Church, but to demonstrate how it actually works. Unfortunately, the leaders of the Roman Catholic Church throughout history have been guilty of extreme forms of crime; abuse of power, fraud, deception, torture and murder. Thereby, they arrogantly ignored every human right which was inconvenient to them.

When presented with issues of life and death (for instance, in the matter of euthanasia) the pope and archbishops immediately take a very moralizing stand.

Would this not be the right time to start an international investigation dealing with the conduct of this institution by a commission of wise (and disinterested) men and women?

Is it not time to negate many opinions of the Roman Catholic Church, especially pertaining to their statements on life and death? Every person is responsible for his own life. However, in general, the fear of death reigns and people do not have the guts to confront life. The hypocritical pronouncements of the Roman Catholic authorities are at odds with the things they have done for centuries, like the killing of people in the most atrocious ways. It would be a credit to these dignitaries if they removed all the smoke and mirrors, which in these days have become irrelevant.

Is it not true that charity is one of the most important pillars of Christian belief? How can it be that the ideal and reality have grown so far apart? When we realize that for centuries religious leaders have preached charity while at the same time practicing greed and elitism, we should be-come doubtful about the Christian theological teachings that have been presented to us, and their doctrines. On which of those, and whose, is it actually based?

I wanted eagerly to get to the core of this and during my quest, my anger continued to grow. I was bewildered! The deceit went far beyond anything I could ever have anticipated. What could have been a beautiful adolescent dream turned into a theological nightmare.

The (False) Truth

From the perspective of the present, I would describe the environment I grew up in as a miniature society, in which the only thing that mattered was to be a Catholic. In those days, there was some segregation in the Netherlands. It is undeniable that in the 1940's and 50's there was not much to do in the Catholic south of the country. North of the big rivers, everything was different. Those regions were inhabited by people who thought differently – by Calvinists or other strict reformists. The churches there always expected people to wear black stockings, which was the symbol of a very strict way of life. That is how we described those people and when we talked about them, it seemed so far away, as if we were speaking of a foreign country. During the war and all it entailed we attached a lot of importance to whatever the pastor preached to us on Sunday. Most people did not have much money to spend and there was an atmosphere of threat and insecurity. Their daily existence was the thing that kept people occupied.

In this world, I grew up in a traditional Catholic family. Sundays, High Mass and Praise were obligatory. The same went for some other days also. We had to attend Praise on Wednesday evening and were obliged to go to church every first Friday of the month. In May and October (the months devoted to Mother Mary), we visited church every night for the rosary prayer. I grew up with themes like the Ten Commandments, and getting indulgence, which we could earn by lighting a candle and reciting, six times, the prayers of Our Father and Hail Mary. After that, we would leave the church for a moment and all would start over again. Every time we followed this routine, we deserved an indulgence on behalf of a deceased person. All devout Catholic persons followed this scheme, because they followed their leaders and believed what the Church taught them. One can compare this to a sect, for the members were brainwashed by their leaders and had their minds turned around. People accepted delusions and fabrications without further investigation. I can still hear my father say, "The pope is infallible in his declarations." It is clear to me that this morbid comedy has been playing for ages. It was most successful during times when common people did not know how to read or write.

In September 1942, my mother took me to school for the first time and I was not exactly eager to go. I was an early pupil, only six years old. With the war raging, there was no such thing as nursery school. During that first year in school, I experienced my First Holy Communion. It was common practice to place the word "holy" before other words, whether it was justified or not. Did this really add any value? Now I know that the Catholic Church wanted this word to convey some sort of elevation, but apart from this woolly, unrealistic theological thinking, the basic meaning of the word *holy* is simply: "complete."

When I grew up it was common practice for the entire first class of a Roman Catholic primary school to be prepared for First Communion. It was not a matter of choice and we simply went with it. Nowadays, parents and child together make the decision whether or not to take First Communion. That is why few children take their First Communion these days. The question arises: who ever came up with this? However, in those days the Church was still the dominant center of society, where people adored the pastor or chaplain of their religious community. It was what people were used to and they were, in a manner of speaking, blind, because nobody noticed the degree of manipulation of this institution called "the Church."

Part of the preparation for First Communion consisted of learning several songs. One of them stuck in my mind. It clearly made a big impression. The first part of the song was, "My Jesus, Beloved Lord, lives behind the golden door of the altar." I remember while I was singing this, it filled me with loathing, but I did not understand why. During visits to the church, the atmosphere of candle light, incense, song and music, was very soothing for me and I would usually drift away into daydreams. Looking at it from my current viewpoint, I think I would have revolted if I had had the capacity to reflect on it, at that time. Utter nonsense of course, Jesus living behind the golden altar door. In my mind, I see the famous Dutch comedian Toon Hermans, telling the public he was knocking on the little door, but nobody ever answered. This is a playful remark, but in fact, it is appalling that even adults did not question this nonsense!

Another example is the Catechism, from which it is clear to what degree we were brainwashed. When I go back in my memory, I still feel anger surging inside me. Looking at it objectively, it is a stupid game of question and answer, which may be appropriate for children, but certainly not for adults. I even wonder if the authors were perhaps children themselves, or if they were simply senile? How many people are still aware of the Catechism? Not many, I presume. This is why I decided to look more closely at this paradigm of the Catholic theological teachings. Quoting some questions and answers:

> To which purpose are we here on earth?
> *We are here on earth in order to serve God and go to heaven.*
>
> Who has taught us how to serve God?
> *Jesus Christ taught us how to serve God.*
>
> How should we obey the teachings of Jesus Christ?
> *We should obey the teachings of Jesus Christ with deep faith and reverence.*
>
> Who is God?
> *God is our Father, who lives in heaven.*

Nowadays we can laugh about a simple game of question and answer like this. Is it not completely ridiculous that they used it to manipulate and brainwash people? Most tragic is that even the teachers believed in this invented nonsense.

The teacher taught us also biblical history and about the Holy Trinity (Father, Son and Holy Ghost) and the confession of faith, which is the Creed of the Catholic Church. Looking back, I now realize the genius of these lessons. The friar knew, acting from his personal religious experience, how to open the hearts of children, in an emotional and almost theatrical way, and then spread the seeds of the Catholic faith. He must have felt great satisfaction, knowing he had fulfilled his task in a splendid manner. The entire class was mesmerized listening to his story and the children looked at the beautiful illustrations of biblical stories that the teacher showed. These friars must have been trained to present their story in a very lively manner. Another example of acting were the preachers, mostly Franciscans or Augustinians, who would often shamelessly conduct the meditations of suffering from the pulpit. They were complete little plays, theatrical to the core.

The friar told us about the Emperor Constantine, who, during one of his hunting parties had seen a deer carrying a shining cross between his antlers. He showed us a beautiful illustration of this occurrence. As a child, I was very susceptible to this kind of story, but I also experienced a feeling of resistance, of doubt about what I was told. During my quest, I concluded that, indeed, many of those beautiful stories they told us were not accurate at all. The subject of the Catholic Church had become an important issue to me in another way: I used it to search for the truth. My curiosity was aroused while reading *The Holy Blood and the Holy Grail*, written by Baigent, Leigh and Lincoln. The book was a revelation to me and at the same time, it confirmed what I already knew. Having conducted research for many years these scientists uncovered secrets that form the basis of our Western civilization. From the first chapter the book intrigued me, and I could not stop reading.

My research consisted, largely, of reading books that discussed in detail the history of the Catholic Church, the papacy and the Bible. However, what I read did not surprise me at all. In most cases, I received images within myself that confirmed what I was reading and formed a supplement to it. My journeys through France and to Rome also supplied me with important information and insights on these subjects. Thus, I discovered that the Roman Catholic Church came into being during a period of great confusion. During the first two centuries C.E., Rome was the center of the European world – a melting pot with people of many nationalities. There were various cults and hundreds of different gods, originating from all kinds of places. The disorder was such that a need began to arise in many minds for a religion centering around one God.

I was intensely interested in all I encountered, but one question kept recurring: Who was this historical figure called Jesus, in reality? It is quite hard to form a coherent idea of him, using biblical texts only.

In the Bible, we read that Jesus was the son of a poor carpenter, born of a virgin, immaculately conceived, and referred to as the Son of God. All very vague and questionable information. All along, it was clear to me that this nonsense simply could not be the truth. Therefore, my quest started with the questions: What is the origin of all this? Moreover, what is the real truth?

I started to look for apocryphal texts (i.e., not approved by the Church), many of which have fortunately been located again after centuries of oblivion. They supply important information.

Despite the fact that the Roman Church destroyed many writings, in order to delete all traces of their deception and malpractice, in 1945 a farmer in Nag Hammadi (Upper Egypt) found a jug. It contained writings dating from the first centuries of Christianity. Scientific research on these texts has shown us that the story of Jesus, as officially presented, is a big lie. Of course, this is sensitive information. I simply feel we should not ignore the truth that finally came to the surface after so many centuries hidden.

Not long after, in 1947, a shepherd found another jug with some very ancient manuscripts, in the caves near Chirbet Qumran, on the northern shore of the Dead Sea. These writings give us a lot of insight into the time when Jesus was born. Several texts show us that Jesus was a rebel. He took exception to the authority of the Roman occupation, but he also did not agree with the orthodox leaders of the Jewish faith.

Both sources confirm that Jesus was a pretender to the throne of David, descended from the old bloodline, and his parents were far from poor. One can draw this conclusion from texts that show his mother associated with other women of importance and fortune. Therefore, Joseph was definitely not a poor carpenter. These documents shed a new light on the origin of Christianity. They give information about the old world, but also about the person of Jesus. They make it easier to understand why the Roman Empire sometimes persecuted the followers of Jesus. To me, the main point is that they show how the Christian faith as we know it today, is based on falsehood. The fact that these texts were found was a miscalculation by the Catholic Church.

In my view, the Bible, especially the New Testament, is no more than a form of literature. It is meant specifically to achieve certain aims by spreading this invented message. Carefully selected texts were combined as if they belonged together. A new sort of theological Christianity had arisen, in which the scholars (exclusively men) played an important part, as "Fathers of the Church."

At the end of the second century C.E., Church Father Irenaeus (bishop of Lyon), selected some evangelical texts from the more than thirty that were current at the time. He chose four, for the simple reason that there were four quarters on a compass. These scriptures were anonymous. It was later on that the names of Mark, Luke, Matthew and John were attached to them. His choices were very sexist: all references to the status of women had to be banished. Writings that did not fit in with his selection were confiscated and burned. There must have been hundreds. Their contents will always remain unknown, but we know they were mostly Gnostic writings, describing the life of Jesus, his marriage to Mary Magdalene and his offspring. The truth had to be disguised.

Irenaeus condemned the followers of Jesus in Nazareth, because they claimed Jesus had been born as a human being and was not of divine descent. Irenaeus proclaimed Jesus had preached the wrong religious teachings and was mistaken in his religious convictions. The Church did everything in its power to reform the life of Jesus in order to make it fit in with the story they claimed was true.

The four gospels as we know them from the New Testament are contradictory. There is the story of Jesus being born in a stable, which we have always been told. It may sound romantic when recited before an open fire and it may have some sentimental value, but it simply cannot be true. Let us look at it with discernment. Matthew and Luke both wrote about the birth and descent of Jesus, but their versions are very different, as well as their time-frames.

According to Matthew, Jesus was an aristocrat, the pretender to the throne of the royal family of David; Luke also mentions Jesus was a descendant of David. Mark, though, tells us the story that the Church sticks to.

Mention of a census during the reign of the first Emperor, Augustus, cannot be found anywhere in historical texts. In all probability, if a census of this stature had taken place, historians would have recorded it. According to Luke this census took place in the year 6 C.E., during the reign of Quirinus, and according to Matthew, Herod died in the year 4 B.C. Obviously, this information is contradictory, because there is a gap of at least nine years.

Luke, who pretended to be a historian, wanted to lend credibility to his story by adding the name of Emperor Augustus. This was usual in those days. However, there was no census in those days: there was a registration in the tax register, which was a regional matter. This was the conclusion of scientific research led by Emil Schürer in 1885. It appeared that the registration was for two different sorts of taxes: personal taxes and property taxes.

These contradictions could never have been solved without the communal archives of the Essenes, as written down in the Dead Sea Scrolls. From them we learn that there were two sorts of birth: first the physical birth (as recounted by Matthew) and then birth into the community, which entailed a ritual rebirth (as noted by Luke). There is a gap of twelve years between the two births. A child then became a member of the Jewish community at the age of thirteen. Luke 2:41-50 says that Jesus, at twelve years old, was detained in the temple and said to his parents, "Didn't you know that I have to be in the house of my Father?" In fact, this refers to twelve years after he became a member of the Jewish community. He was 24 years old and had to discuss his status with the teachers of the temple. Here his "Father" refers to his religious father, the high priest, the "father" of the Jewish community.

In those times, two systems of dating were used, the Roman and the Hebrew, and this is the cause of some confusion. We know that Jesus was born during the reign of King Herod the Great, so this must have been before his death in 4 B.C.

The occurrence on Jesus' 24th birthday in the temple gives us the exact month of his birth. Luke states it was during Easter. Jews celebrate Easter in March, which is the first month of the Hebrew calendar. According to the Essene dating system the term for every first day of the month was this day, or "today." Luke 2:11 says, "Today a savior was born in the city of David." Judging from the difference between the Hebrew and Roman calendars, Jesus was born on March 1, in the year 7 B.C.

Neither Jesus nor his parents could have lived in Nazareth, a town that did not even exist in those days. Nazareth is not noted on old maps and historians do not make any mention of it. Jesus was called "the Nazarene," but this was because he was a member of the society of the Nazarene.

The name Nazareth stems from the Hebrew word Nazrie ha-Brit, which was the name of an Essene community. Therefore, "Jesus of Nazareth" never existed.

So, where did he actually live? Joseph came from Bethlehem and lived there, so it seems logical that Jesus lived there too. This is the most obvious conclusion, because Bethlehem was the town of King David, of whom Jesus was a direct descendant. Why would the Romans make a registration of Joseph in the tax register, if he did not live in Bethlehem and was not affluent? Because of this, the story of the inn must be false as well. If a person owns a home in Bethlehem, why not sleep there in comfort, rather than stay at an inn, instead? The mention of a "carpenter," walking beside a donkey on which his heavily pregnant wife was seated has to be taken in the symbolic sense. It is a fabricated story. Just like the story of the virgin birth in a stable or cave. This simply seemed to fit in. The same goes for the shepherds with their sheep, the singing angels and the miserable conditions. It is absurd! Research shows that Jesus was the son of wealthy parents, both of whom were of royal blood: Joseph was born into the House of David and Mary belonged to an Armenian dynasty.

The Catholic Church wants us to believe that the conception of Jesus happened by divine intervention, a visiting angel. This too is complete nonsense. Of course, Joseph and Mary conceived the child in the natural way. From Essene writings, it is known that the "coming in of the soul" was viewed as supernatural. Luke describes it as the Holy Spirit.

Joseph and Mary had more children: the Bible, as well as other writings, mentions that Jesus had brothers and sisters. We know about James,

Thomas (Didymus), Joseph, Simon, Judas, Sarah-Salome, Joanna, and Mary (wife of Cleopas).

In the Bible, we read that Jesus was standing on the shore of the lake of Galilee and said to the fishermen Peter and Andrew, "Come, and follow me." This text wants us to believe that a following of twelve apostles came into being in this manner. It's another lie, because these apostles were no fishermen. It is very naïve to believe this, because when somebody tells someone else to "come and follow me," would they miraculously turn away from their profession and family, just like that? Nice fabrication, but not very realistic. In the Essene writings, we find that there were indeed twelve apostles, but they were more like political representatives of Jesus. Their task was to recruit followers for their cause. When a number of people wished to join them, they were invited to the joining ceremony. This can be compared to joining a political party and the taking of the oath that follows. The ceremony consisted of all new members immersing themselves in the water, after which, they were literally fished up in nets by the apostles. After that, these non-Jews were included in the Jewish traditions. Therefore, the apostles were "fishers of people." They were not poor, illiterate, professional fishermen, as the Church would like us to believe. The procedure the Messiah followed was part of the Jewish law. Among the apostles were his brothers James, Thomas, and Judas, as well as Simon-Lazarus, Peter and Philip.

The Bible tells us that Jesus performed miracles, made the lame walk, made the blind see and so on. But were they really miracles? Jesus was a healer, trained by the Essenes, who knew a lot about natural healing. He supplied the ailing with energy and power, in order to stimulate their energetic circulation. This is more or less the same kind of medicine the Greeks practiced around 400 B.C. Hippocrates of Cos and his followers applied their hands to people's bodies to incite healing and made use of medicinal herbs. This practice is still in sway and there is no need of miracles! I think back on my own practice, where I would treat people who were bent-over by sciatica. I helped the energy flow and distracted them, in order to break through the mental spiral they were in. Afterwards they would walk upright again, free of pain. The medical world would look upon a recovery like this as a miraculous event, but it is certainly no miracle in the sense meant by the Church.

The gospels tell us about the Last Supper. This is false too! Having the status of Messiah, Jesus was obliged to host a Messianic Banquet at least once a year, with the twelve representatives. This event was twisted, and the biblical version of the Last Supper came into being. The mythical images of bread and wine were added later.

The hypocritical fathers of Roman Catholicism were convinced they had destroyed the (inconvenient) truth. Fortunately, those old writings were saved (a miracle?) and later came to the surface.

In one of these, the gospel of Philip, we read that Jesus mostly held company with three women: his mother Mary, his sister Sarah-Salome and Mary Magdalene, his companion. Jesus loved Mary Magdalene in a different way. He used to kiss her on the mouth in the presence of disciples. The others witnessed his love for Mary and asked him, "Why do you love her more than any of us?" Jesus answered, "Why I do not love you, the way I love her? Well, if a blind person and a person with sight are in the dark together, there is no difference between them. But when the light emerges, the person with sight will see the light and the blind person has to remain in the dark." The fact that Jesus kissed her on the mouth means there was intimacy between them. Jesus treated Mary Magdalene like a partner, in a physically loving way.

According to the Nag Hammadi library, Mary Magdalene acted as an intermediary between Jesus and his disciples, who did not always understand what he intended to convey. Despite the fact that it was unusual for a woman, in those days, to come to the fore, Jesus encouraged her to speak. He praised her abundantly and openly. This was hard to take in for the apostles, being used to a male-dominated culture. Some disciples called her "the woman who knows the All." This means either Jesus informed Mary Magdalene about the cosmic laws, or perhaps she was wise in her own right.

On very old icons from Middle and South Europe, the painters depicted her as a teacher among twelve men, the apostles.

The Gospel of Thomas, also found in the jug at Nag Hammadi, confirms that Jesus was intimate with Mary Magdalene.

In the Gospel of the Roman Church, there is reference to Jesus expelling seven demons from Mary Magdalene. They mean seven evil spirits. This is a lie, a distortion of the truth. The Nag Hammadi library makes it clear that she received seven *initiations* from Jesus. Mary Magdalene, as a woman, lived in the near vicinity of Jesus and this would only be possible if she were a near relative, like a cousin, or even a wife.

According to the Nag Hammadi library, the apostles called Mary Magdalene *apostola apostolorum*, meaning the apostle to the apostles. Peter had difficulty accepting her position and he even threatened to kill her.

He could not accept the fact that a woman took the first place next to Jesus, instead of one of the male apostles. The other apostles also regarded her as inferior.

In the orthodox Jewish tradition, the man is considered superior. The woman lost her status of being equal to the man, which she had in the Essene tradition. Peter was not fond of women and the fact that Mary Magdalene was the wife of Jesus, was mostly repressed. In the Bible, Paul proclaimed that women were not allowed to speak in church. They could not claim their part in whatever function men held.

In the beginning, Christianity was largely a movement following Jewish ways. The first Christians were usually from Jewish origin and held onto many traditional viewpoints. During the second century, a process of separation came about in the Church: the men were responsible for the ritual side and the women revered in silence. Quintus Tertullianus, a Church father with the style of Paul, took measures at the end of the second century to ensure that women were no longer involved in the Church. They were not allowed to officially engage in religious practice and if they did so anyway, they were called a whore or a witch.

In the authentic early Christian texts, we also read that Mary Magdalene and Jesus had three children. This goes to show how brazen the Church was in adapting the scriptures and committing fraud.

In the Gnostic tradition, Mary Magdalene was surrounded by wisdom. In Greek, "sophia" was symbolized as the sun, the moon and a shining wreath of stars. It was also referred to as "the complete spirit." This is very different from the Holy Spirit, the translation propagated by the Church. Later on, they connected this shining wreath of stars to Jesus' mother, the other Mary. With the fabrication of the Father, Son and the Holy Spirit (the so-called Divine Trinity), everything was taken completely out of context in order to fit in with the new dogma of the Apostolic Church of Peter, whose viewpoints are clearly brought forward in the Gospel of Thomas, in which he seriously objects to the presence of Mary Magdalene in Jesus' following. In the Gospel of Mary Magdalene, Peter doubts her relationship to Jesus. "Would he really have spoken intimately with a woman, and not with us? Why should we change our minds and listen to her?"

In "Pistis Sophia," Peter complains about Mary's participation and he asks Jesus to keep her from undermining his superiority.

It became more and more clear to me that Jesus wanted to lead his people in great wisdom, but his chauvinistic political rivals rendered this impossible.

This was the reason Jesus' mission against the Roman rule in Judah and the uprising he instigated failed. The sectarian Jews were divided amongst themselves and he received support only from the Nazarenes and the Essene community. Out of self-interest, the Hebrew faction and the Sanhedrin (Council of Elders) withheld their support. They were content with their important positions within the Roman administration. In this manner, the Romans could restrain this troublesome part of their empire without much effort. They corrupted the religious leaders with power and money. This made it much more difficult for the people to revolt; tend to use an obscure system of control.

The Romans had objections to Jesus' polemics, because he proclaimed that the Jewish god was also the god of the non-Jews. That is why his followers did not get the support of the orthodox Jewish establishment and the Romans treated them as a nuisance.

Historian Flavius Josephus wrote in the year 70 that there were, among the Jews, several philosophical factions. The cultures of these communities differed greatly in many aspects. The Essenes were liberal and affectionate. They pursued mysticism and gnosis, believed in the Messiah and followed the teachings of the prophet Elijah. Their community bore a resemblance to a monastery. They practiced Egyptian healing and were therefore referred to as *Therapeutae*. The Nazarene community formed a subsect to the Essenes. Paul became one of their foremost leaders.

When I read that Jesus had survived the crucifixion because of a scheme made up by James, and that his wounds were healed by Simon the Zealot (a magician), this agreed totally with a text I had read elsewhere. The text dealt with several discoveries made in southeastern France about the history of the Cathars. This text, and what I discovered during my trips to this region and the images that came to me there, confirm this scheme. More about this later.

The Gospel of Mark was written in a period when the Jews revolted against the rule of the Roman Empire in 66 C.E. The Romans did not hesitate to kill rebels. Emperor Nero was unreliable and it is with good reason that he is often referred to as a cruel lunatic. Two years prior to this, Herod of Chalcis captured Peter and he was taken to Rome. Paul also fell into disgrace and was captured too. The Emperor Nero executed both. Peter was crucified upside down, according to his own wishes, because he wanted to show how the arrival of Jesus turned all relations upside down. At the same time, Paul was decapitated. Many Catholics see Peter as the first pope, but this is complete nonsense. In the year 64, there was no such thing as a hierarchical Church. I am not surprised that people think like this. It just shows again that leaders of the Church misinformed their believers in many ways.

During the 2nd century, Church Father Clemens of Alexandria confirmed these Roman cruelties. This meant that Mark had to express himself in a certain way, to make sure he would not come into conflict with the occupying forces. In order to survive he had no other option than to twist the truth! That led to the myth that Jesus lived in poverty and, for example, we are not told that he was fiercely against the Roman occupier. If Mark had written a truthful story, he would not have survived!

Because of this, his scripture is unreliable, even though the Church has marked it as a Holy Gospel. The essential meaning of the word holy is whole or complete. This concept has been completely taken out of its context.

The Gospel of Mark holds elements that are missing completely from the old Greek texts. When the New Testament was compiled, during the 4th century, this Gospel ended with chapter 16:8. This we can conclude from the Codex Vaticanus and the Codex Sinaiticus, kept in the archives of the Vatican. The verses that have been added to chapter 16 are completely different in literary style. Mark 16:9 repeats the text of Luke 8:2 in a subtle way. The reader is reminded of the seven demons of Mary Magdalene and in this way the Church degrades her status of "apostle to the apostles' once again. Mark 16:15 speaks of the apostles being sent to all corners of the world to spread the good news everywhere. This was a strategy meant to sideline Mary Magdalene and other women.

In 1958 Morton Smith drew up a catalogue of the monastery in Mar Saba near Qumran. In a book written by Ignatius of Antioch from the first century, he discovered a letter that Church father, Clemens of Alexandria, had sent to his colleague Theodore. This letter contained a short version taken from the Gospel of Mark, which had been omitted since then from verse 16:9. This letter commissions Theodore to remove this part of the gospel and to keep silent about it, because it was not consistent with the course that had been agreed. These agreements had to do with the status of Mary Magdalene and with women in general. The letter noted,

> If someone speaks the truth, we should not agree, because the truth, we now know from this faith, is the only truth. If it becomes known that things have been falsified, we should never admit that it is about the secret Gospel of Mark. It is better

to deny this under oath, because not all that is true should be divulged to the people.

The missing part of the gospel recounts that Roman governor Pontius Pilate had used state funds for his own purposes. He was charged in 32 C.E., but his soldiers killed the accusers. What followed was an armed revolt, led by Simon the Zealot. The revolt went amiss, and King Herod-Agrippa declared Simon an outlaw. According to Jewish law, this was much the same as a death sentence. The castaway would be undressed, placed in a shroud and confined to a crypt. Mary and Martha knew that if he was not pardoned (resurrected) within three days, then on the fourth day, the sentence would be executed, his soul cursed forever. Therefore, they sent the message to Jesus that Simon was ill. Jesus did not know what to do. He was powerless, because only a priest could perform a resurrection. Jesus then decided that he would take the role of a priest upon him and liberated Simon. During this period, dissension arose between Herod-Agrippa and the Roman authorities. Herod-Agrippa was forced to pass his legal power on to his uncle Herod-Antipas, who annulled Simon's status of outlaw, for the simple reason that he had supported the revolt of the Zealots. Jesus had violated the rules, but Herod-Antipas forced the high priest to accept this *fait accompli*. People saw this as a miracle, because normally Jesus should have been put to death, following Jewish law. The high priest and the Pharisees did not accept that this breach of the rules went unpunished. From that moment on they consulted with each other, devising a way to kill Jesus.

About the status of Jesus and whether he was married or not, we only know that, according to Jewish custom, it would be a disgrace if he was not married. In that case, the historians would certainly have mentioned this.

The missing piece of the Gospel of Mark deals with Lazarus, who called out to Jesus from within his crypt, even before the stone was rolled away. This shows clearly that he was not dead and that this had nothing to do with a supernatural miracle.

The difference between John and Mark is in the behavior of Mary Magdalene. John says, "When Mary Magdalene heard that Jesus was on the way, she went out to meet him." The missing part of Mark states that Mary stayed at home, until Martha came to tell her that Jesus was asking for her. At that moment, she left her home and went to meet Jesus.

Being a married woman, she was bound to the strict code of marital habits and therefore she had to wait for permission to leave her home.

Clemens of Alexandria wanted to delete this text, because it was proof that Jesus and Mary Magdalene were married.

From this text, it also becomes clear that Lazarus, friend of Jesus and subject of the story we know from the Bible, was the same person as Simon the Zealot, also known as Simon the Pharisee. According to Mark and Matthew, Mary Magdalene anointed Jesus in Bethania, in the home of Simon the Leper, former Pharisee. John mentions "in the home of Lazarus."

In this period, people commonly had several names or titles. This caused mix-ups later on, and the omitting of parts of the text in order to hide the truth only added to the confusion. In this way, it is clear that objectivity is nowhere to be found and that the current gospels cannot be considered reliable. Therefore, it is remarkable that the Gospels of Matthew and Luke elaborate on the Gospel of Mark, written by John Mark (a colleague of Paul) in 66 C.E. The Gospel of Luke originated in 80 C.E. in Antioch and five years later, the Gospel of Matthew was drawn up in Corinth.

So, the situation was like this: around the year 80, everything still had to be written down, with the Gospel of Mark acting as the source, and Mark had not been at liberty to tell the truth.

The Gospel of John, however, is different from the other three. The contents and style show a strong influence from the Essene tradition. A very noteworthy difference is the position of Mary – this Gospel hardly mentioned her.

It starts with, "In the beginning was the Word, and the Word was with God." "The Word" referred to Jesus. In Acts 8:14 it says that the inhabitants of Samaria had accepted the Word of God, meaning that Jesus was at that time in Samaria. Acts 6:7 says, "So the Word of God spread," meaning that more and more people listened to what Jesus had to say.

Oddly enough, the wedding of Cana, where Jesus performed his first miracle by changing water into wine, can only be found in the Gospel of John. Jesus had no sympathy whatsoever for the strict religious beliefs of the Pharisees and he knew that the people of Judah could not be liberated from the Roman oppression unless they let go of their obstinate fanaticism. He also realized that they had been waiting for their prophesied holy man for a long time; a Messiah, who would deliver them from the Romans and herald a new era of liberation. As the heir of the House of King David, he definitely qualified for this and it would not have surprised anybody if he had claimed this role. He had revolutionary ideas and wanted to distance himself from the orthodox habits.

In the social field, he had no authority; he was neither an anointed king nor a high priest. He disregarded that technicality, though. Despite his unofficial status, he overturned many of the Hebrew traditions.

Miracles are not necessarily paranormal events, but of course, they do count as special and unprecedented. It is confusing when you often encounter words that, purposely or not, have been translated wrongly. Knowing that biblical texts were subject to much falsification, to me it is safe to conclude that this was no accident. In this case the word "*dunameis*" was mistranslated into "a miracle," even though it refers to "an action of power," which is sometimes equal to surprise.

At the wedding of Cana, when Jesus had the opportunity to openly break with the convention for the first time, he hesitated and said, "My time has not come yet." His mother brushed aside his lack of authority and told the servants "Do whatever he tells you to do, no matter what." When the wine had nearly run out, Mary told her son about the shortage. Then it appears he changed water into wine. According to the Dead Sea Scrolls, it was the custom that serving wine was reserved for the priest in charge. Jesus had no priestly authority, so his dealing with the wine situation would mean a violation of this rule. Only fully initiated Levites were allowed to drink ceremonial wine. All others present were seen as uninitiated and could only do a ritual cleansing with water. *Others* included married men, converts, non-Jews and all non-priestly Jews.

John 2:6 says, "Now there were six stone water jars for Jewish ceremonial washings, each holding twenty to thirty gallons." Jesus broke with the tradition by ignoring the cleansing water and allowing the uninitiated guests to drink the holy wine. The master of ceremonies did not know where the wine came from, but he did not speak of a miracle. He made a remark about the good wine being served to the guests at that late stage of the party. Mary declared, this showed the greatness of Jesus, and his disciples believed in him.

Cana was not about a wedding ceremony; in fact, it was an engagement meal. Some disciples attended and there were all kinds of guests. The official host, as the master of ceremonies, was in charge of the procedure and second in command were the groom and his mother. No guest ever had the right to give orders. Because of the fact that Jesus and his mother both gave orders to the servants, many theologians feel this proves that Jesus and the groom were the same person.

John Shelby Spong, Bishop of Newark, also agrees with them. Based on the wedding in Cana and 1 Corinthians 1:5 he poses the following questions concerning the wives and sisters of the apostles that escorted Jesus:

> How comes it Mary Magdalene was considered the most important
> of this group of women (the apostle to the apostles), her name al-
> ways being mentioned first, if she is not Jesus' wife? Why does this
> woman have the right to claim the body of Jesus (John 20:15) if she
> is not related to him? Why would she take upon herself the task of
> anointing the body of Jesus, the task of a wife, if she is not his wife?

He concluded that Jesus and Mary Magdalene were husband and wife.
Rome has kept this fact silent, but it was not deleted.

From certain texts, we can conclude that the wedding in Cana was dated
in June of the year 30 C.E. This dating is fitting for a dynastic engagement
celebration, being three months before the first marriage in September. In
September of this same year, Mary Magdalene anointed Jesus (the marriage
ceremony) in the home of Simon. In this same period, she was also said to
have wept for her husband (Luke 7:38), before being separated from him
until November, according to the law. After that, she was referred to as "a
crippled woman," the term used for "a young woman who is engaged."

I went from one surprise to the next and my suspicions were very
much confirmed.

In the Bible, it says that Jesus loved one disciple more than he loved
any other. I kept wondering who this person was.

For centuries, the "disciple Jesus loved most" has been a mystery and
the subject of much debate. For a long time, people thought this referred
to John, but Mary Magdalene and John Mark also held a high score.

The only biblical reference to this can be found in the Gospel of John.
At the crucifixion, Jesus appointed this "Beloved Disciple" as the one to
take care of his mother. In this text, Mary Magdalene cannot be the subject, for it speaks of a man. In the text about the resurrection, on the way
to the crypt, this same disciple appears together with Peter. Again, this
excludes Mary Magdalene, for she spoke to this disciple.

It is strange that the author of the Gospel of John was not clear about
something so important. Yet, one passage shows that Jesus was very fond
of one of his male disciples in particular, noted at the resurrection of
Lazarus, "Jesus loved Mary, her sister Martha, and Lazarus very much."
After the resurrection, the Jews present said, "He loved him so much."

Therefore, the disciple referred to must have been Lazarus, alias Simon
the Zealot. He was the disciple Jesus loved most. Besides being an apostle,
Simon was also the chief of the Qumran community and member of Jesus' family, who had good reason to place his mother in the care of Simon.

Who is, in fact, the author of the Gospel of John?

The author of the Book of Revelation is introduced as John the Apostle; however, the text is anonymous, not from the same hand as Revelation and was not written by the author of the Epistles of John. The author of the gospel knew many details, was informed about many priestly customs, and had a close relationship to Jesus.

At the end, it says that the source of all this information is "the disciple Jesus loved, although he is not the author." In John 21:24 it says: "This is the disciple who testifies to these things and who wrote them down. We know that his testimony is true." Therefore, this is not the testimony of John, but that of Simon the Zealot, who first supplied the information to the author of this gospel.

The story itself provides some information as to the identity of the author. In all four Gospels Mary Magdalene is present at Jesus' crypt. She was the only one who had to be there, in order to anoint her husband. Contrary to the other gospels, this document states that she was alone at the crypt. It also describes the personal conversation between Jesus and Mary Magdalene. Apart from these two, nobody else was present, so one of them must be the author. Therefore, Mary Magdalene has to be the author of this gospel, unless it was Jesus himself.

The Church Fathers knew this and so did Jerome, which is why they claimed the author was John.

The Roman Catholic Church is, after all, responsible for this kind of forgery. I will give more examples that are unknown to most people.

During the 4th century, Bishop Athanasius of Alexandria, following his own judgment, selected writings that, in his opinion, matched very well. A short while after this, Pope Damasus I commissioned the Roman Church scholar Jerome to check these texts, written in Latin, and to make sure they were consistent. This resulted in Jerome making more than 3500 alterations in the texts of the Old and New Testaments. He also commissioned monks to write new material, to fill up the gaps.

These fraudulent alterations resulted in the biblical manuscripts, like the Codex Alexandrinus and the later on discovered Codex Sinaiticus; both written in Greek. The Latin version was derived from these, called Codex Vaticanus.

After this forgery, the texts were submitted to the Council of Hippo in 393 and that of Carthage in 397. Everything had been prepared in detail. Because of the strategy that was taken, approval by both councils was no more than a formality. In fact, they laid the foundation for the Bible as we know it, the so-called infallible Word of God.

Throughout the centuries, people kept altering the remaining texts meticulously, following the conduct that started with Emperor Constantine.

The Gospel of John, contrary to the other Gospels, devotes a lot of attention to the suffering and crucifixion of Jesus.

It is important to know if they indeed crucified Jesus, and if so, whether he died while on the cross. I can imagine Jesus being crucified, but I have always had my doubts about him dying on the cross. Especially when I found out that documents had been discovered in France, which contain direct evidence that Jesus lived in France and died there. This confirmed my suspicions and took away my doubts. Based on the existing story from the New Testament, the only possible conclusion is that it is a deceit. In the Gospels, Jesus was depicted as a non-political person. The only possible reason for the Romans to put him to death is if he conducted a crime against them, but the evangelists tell us that he abided by the law as decreed by the occupying forces. We know the orthodox Jews were ill-disposed toward him, but if he was condemned according to Jewish law, he could only be stoned.

The details of the crucifixion, for example, had to be described as the Old Testament had predicted them. Church Father Jerome took care of this, let there be no doubt about that. The forgers omitted certain details and twisted texts around in order to make the story consistent. In those days, the great majority did not speak up for themselves (without risking terrible consequences) and were illiterate, so it was easy to make them believe anything.

Scientists are clearly divided about the crucifixion. It has been ascertained, from the many investigations into his historical character, that Jesus was indeed crucified by the Romans because he spoke against their dominion. This sort of resistance, organized meetings, and outright rebellion were punished with flogging and/or crucifixion.

The Gospel of John gives a detailed report of the crucifixion – and therefore it seems more reliable than the other three. It says for example that Jesus had thirst and was offered a sponge drenched in vinegar, which was brought to his mouth on a pike. Vinegar, among its many qualities, was used medicinally to revive people who had fainted. However, Jesus reacted in a completely different manner. He spoke some last words and seemed to pass away.

The fact that they wanted to break Jesus' legs was a sign of impatience – he had a pedestal under his feet. If he had hung only by his wrists, he would have suffocated in minutes. Joseph of Arimathea, however, enjoyed great privileges from the Romans. Because the crucifixion took place on his own terrain, he intervened and prevented the breaking of Jesus' legs.

According to John 19:34, blood and water flowed from the wound, after a soldier had thrust his lance into Jesus' side. This is generally taken as a sign that he was dead, but the vascular bleeding indicates he was not.

What was really soaked into that sponge? In those days, anesthetic drugs like belladonna and opium were readily available. Joseph of Arimathea may have chosen one of these to make the Romans believe Jesus was dead, and get permission to take him from the cross, all facilitated by the fact that the crucifixion took place on his own land. The apostles, it seems, were not in on the caper. They, too, believed that Jesus was dead – and it saved his life.

Joseph of Arimathea helped fulfill the old scriptures, in the same way Church Father Jerome has done. Jesus had to rise from death after three days. It is obvious that the crucifixion did not take place on Golgotha, for this is a bare hill shaped like a skull, to the northeast of Jerusalem. The Gospel of John states that the site of the crucifixion was a garden of olive trees. By adding the name Golgotha and twisting some words, the story becomes completely different. The Book of Revelation 11:8 states that Jesus was crucified in "the great city that is figuratively called Sodom and Egypt." The Therapeutae called Qumran "Egypt" and this place was geographically associated with the town of Sodom.

The afore-mentioned crypt belonged to a family in the garden of Joseph of Arimathea. Discovered in 1947, it was called *the cave of the rich man*. Jesus' body was placed in the main room, showing that his family must have been quite prominent and affluent.

Who, in fact, was Joseph of Arimathea?

In the Gospel of Mark, we find that he was "a prominent councilor (a member of the Sanhedrin), who also expected the arrival of the Kingdom of God." According to John he was "a secret disciple of Jesus, for he feared the Jews." Yet his connection to Jesus was not surprising to the Roman governor Pontius Pilate. He granted Joseph permission, without question, to take Jesus' body down from the cross and place it in the family crypt. Aside from that, Jesus' mother, his sisters Mary and Sarah-Salome and Mary Magdalene all agreed to the way Joseph took care of things.

From the apocryphal writings, it is clear that Joseph of Arimathea, Jesus' brother, James, and James the Just, were the same person: somebody who had a lot of influence and was far from poor.

Joseph of Arimathea was a given title, which indicated a very high status. The name Arimathea was a combination of Hebrew and Greek elements: "ha rama" (of altitude) and "theo" (referring to God). The personal title was His Divine Highness.

Jesus was successor to the throne in the line of David, so he was referred to as "the David." The title "the Joseph" was assigned to the successor who was then next in line to the throne. When a dynastic son from the House of Judah became the David (king), his oldest son became "the Joseph." If at this time he had no son, or if his son was younger than sixteen, the eldest brother of the David was given the title of Joseph, which he would then pass on when the son had reached the required age. James was the oldest of Jesus' younger brothers and this is why he became the Joseph ha Rama Theo, which was transposed into Joseph of Arimathea.

When I discovered all of this, I was very happy, for it became more and more clear to me that my doubts were justified. It is all so very logical, especially since the scrolls that were discovered in southeastern France in the 19th century also confirmed this information.

Simon the Zealot, who was after all a magician, had installed himself inside the crypt to take care of Jesus. John 19:39 states that Nicodemus arrived next, with "a mixture of myrrh and aloe, some hundred litra." Extract of myrrh helps to calm a person down and aloe juice is a fast-working purging agent. This was exactly what Simon needed in order to dispel the poison from Jesus' body.

It is important to note that the day after the crucifixion was the Sabbath. The timing of Jesus' revival depended on the exact time in which the Sabbath started. In those days, there were twelve hours in the day and twelve hours in the night, but time had to be adjusted when the days/nights became longer or shorter. That Friday, time had to be adjusted by three hours (ahead). This makes for a discrepancy between the reports of Mark and John. Mark follows the solar system and John uses the lunar system. The key is in these three missing hours – the daytime hours were turned into nighttime hours. The Samaritan wise men used an astronomical timetable and changed the time three hours later. In this way, Simon had three full hours at his disposal to care for Jesus, without having to violate the rules that prohibited working on the Sabbath.

In the early morning of the day after Sabbath, Mary Magdalene noticed that Jesus was no longer inside the crypt and went searching for him. She saw a man in the garden who she presumed was Joseph of Arimathea, but soon discovered it was Jesus himself.

What kind of woman would not immediately want to kiss and hold her husband, seeing him alive when she thought he was dead? However, Jesus ordered her not to embrace him. This meant that Mary Magdalene was pregnant, because physical contact between husband and wife during pregnancy was not allowed at that time.

Of course, Joseph of Arimathea explained his plans to her afterwards.

According to Acts 1:16-18, the traitor, Judas Iscariot, was relentlessly pushed over the edge of a cliff. The Roman Church claimed that Judas hanged himself, but this story is not based on anything but their imagination.

After the crucifixion, confusion reigned. Nobody knew Jesus was still alive, because it would pose a threat from the orthodox Jews.

After the conviction of Jesus, the Romans managed to regain control over the rebellious province of Judah. The Roman emperor had done all within his power to bend the religious leaders of the Jews to his will. He made sure they felt important by offering them positions of authority, for instance, as "Councillor to the King of Jerusalem."

During the reign of King Herod-Agrippa I in the year 43, his councillors decided that all followers of Jesus were revolutionaries. They misled the king by warning him that this movement was dangerous and that the group intended to overthrow the priests of the temple, who acted as the legal authorities. This was the cause for the first persecutions of Jesus' followers. The king took severe action and captured and punished many people.

James and his Nazarenes became a great threat to the Roman authorities in Jerusalem. Because of this, King Agrippa's brother, the King of Chalcis in the year 44, killed the Apostle James (brother of John).

Simon the Zealot was one of Jesus' apostles, but he was also known as a fanatic. He immediately sought revenge and had King Herod-Agrippa poisoned. He then had to flee. The Apostle Thaddeus tried also to escape but was captured and killed.

Simon's assault had everything to do with an uprising he had conducted in the year 32, against Pontius Pilate. Because of this, Herod-Agrippa I declared him an outlaw. The members of the Sanhedrin and the Roman authorities, both having played an important role in the prosecution and conviction of Jesus, searched for Simon and held suspicions with regard to his kindred spirits. The pregnant Mary Magdalene found herself in a dangerous situation, because Herod of Chalcis knew she was in touch with Simon. She was a relative of Simon as well as a fellow believer and was suspected of having joined the Zealots.

Mary Magdalene, who was married to Jesus, had to give birth to a family heir in order to maintain the line of descent of David. She was successful, for her second child was a son. After this birth and the prescribed period of separation, Jesus and Mary continued their marriage in December of 43 AD. She fell pregnant for the third time and soon after, in the spring of 44, Jesus left for Galatia (a Roman province in Asia Minor). He left because the Jewish tradition prescribed married people to live apart during pregnancy and for a certain period following the birth. The important proselyte (someone who is converted to Judaism) John Mark travelled with him.

Mary Magdalene also played a key role in the network of the apostles, which had started to spread its activities into other countries.

The term *christiani* (followers of Jesus) was used for the first time in the year 44, in Antioch, and this is where the new religion developed, before it spread to Rome.

Since Peter was Jesus' right-hand man, he would have to act as protector of Mary Magdalene during the time of their separation. Despite the fact that Peter himself was married, he despised women and was not prepared to wait hand and foot on a priestess who challenged his authority. He prevented Mary Magdalene from reaching a position of any importance in Antioch.

After the king's death by poisoning, many apostles and disciples fled from Judah, fearing revenge. Many reached Rome, where they joined with the members of the Roman School, who had accepted Jesus' teachings. Those who could not escape were captured and executed.

Simon the Zealot and Mary Magdalene had to leave Judah in any case and this is why Mary was placed under his care.

Herod-Agrippa II (a former pupil of Paul) protected Mary and this is how they arranged their passage to Herod's country estate near Vienne, north of Marseille. Simon the Zealot led the company that, among others, consisted of the pregnant Mary Magdalene and her two children, Sarah-Tamar and Jesus, and some wealthy ladies we could call ladies-in-waiting. This company arrived in Gaul and the Queen of Marseille welcomed them. In 1526, Pera Matas splendidly captured this event in a painting. In the Provence, one can find many religious works of art, depicting the boat journey of Mary Magdalene, as well as her speaking to the local residents.

Philip had arranged with James, Jesus' brother, to meet in Gaul, together with Jesus. The British monk and historian Gildas Sapiens reported this in the 6th century.

Imperial documents, stemming from the time before the Roman Church originated, mention the Greek word "*Desposyni*," a word that was reserved only for those who were related to Jesus. Father Malachi Martin, a Jesuit, who worked in the Vatican at the beginning of the 20th century, confirmed this later. During his studies there, he discovered the many lies by the Church after which he left the Society of Jesus in 1964 and turned his back on the Church completely.

Nevertheless, despite the confusion that arose around the crucifixion of Jesus and the persecution by the Romans, more and more people embraced Jesus' teachings, which resulted in a large group of followers. They organized meetings in Rome and kept their faith alive in the catacombs. In Rome, and throughout the Empire, they formed groups and conducted their ceremonies in secret. The apostles and their pupils, who had known Jesus in person, took the lead. They organized and maintained the contacts between the different groups.

Due to their stubborn intransigence, the Romans sometimes persecuted the *christiani* ruthlessly and committed many atrocities. Many followers were executed, forced to fight the gladiators in the Roman Colosseum, or were literally thrown to the lions, gruesome atrocities that were unprecedented in religious matters.

I devoured every book that dealt with the origin of Christianity and in this way, it became clear to me that there were two factions in the early days:

On the one hand were the Nazarenes, led by Jesus' brother James. Among the members were Simon the Zealot, Philip, Thomas, Thaddeus, Sarah-Salome (Jesus' sister) and Mary Magdalene.

On the other hand, there was the evangelical school of Peter, which had its base in Rome. It was an independent group but in the long term, it deviated from Jesus' original purposes.

In these early days, we find all kinds of symbols and allegories. (An allegory is a symbol that hides its true meaning.) They were metaphors, used to protect the early Christians from the Romans. The vine, for instance, was used as a symbol of life and growth, but also of the family tree. The vine brought forth the grape. In the Bible, this is a metaphor for "go forth and multiply." Jesus stated that he was the true vine and continued the line of David, because he was the successor to the throne.

I also discovered that the Church Fathers Valentine and Mark, who adhered to the Gnostic teaching of Jesus, declared in the year 150 that wine was a metaphor for the royal heritage of Jesus and not a metaphor for his blood.

The persecution of the *christiani* continued into the 4th century, when the arrival of a new emperor, Constantine the Great, turned the tide.

Constantine was a believer in monotheism (the belief that there is only one God). Like his father, he worshipped the sun god, Sol Invictus.

He merged several features of the *christiani* with elements of the sun cult. The result was a hybrid religion that finally grew into what we call the Roman Catholic Church.

From his youth Constantine learned about Christianity, in which he showed more and more interest. This interest does not justify the conclusion that he identified with the Christian belief system, because he did not organize his own baptism until he was on his deathbed. Nevertheless, he credited his victories to the god of the *christiani*.

In October 312, Constantine defeated his rival Maxentius in the Battle of the Milvian Bridge, which lay to the north of Rome. This conquest made him the unrivalled ruler of the West. Four months later, he declared his "Edict of Tolerance" in Milan, which gave the *christiani*, among others, total freedom to practice their religion. He was a political genius. The new emperor understood that the empire would be wrecked by the endless struggle against the followers of Jesus. From that moment on, the persecution and punishing of the *christiani* ended.

The new emperor did not capitulate to Christianity, he provided freedom to the Christians only in order to abuse this situation later on. Therefore, he had to maintain strict control. This change forced the bishops to learn how to deal with their newfound position in the state and to cultivate some sort of diplomacy. The emperor garlanded the bishops with gold and upgraded their function enormously. By doing this, he made them dependent and submissive. The bishops looked up to the emperor and felt very flattered. The church authorities of those days embraced the freedom and wealth they received from Constantine.

In January 314, Sylvester became the Bishop of Rome and he stayed in position for 21 years. Constantine appointed him the prime bishop of his empire and bestowed upon him the Lateran Palace, from that moment on the official residence of the Bishop of Rome.

Sylvester followed Constantine's directions and did not develop any initiatives of his own. Of course, the emperor welcomed this situation, because he was determined to turn Christianity into a valuable political instrument. Constantine left religious problems to the courts of the Church, to which he gave the same authority as the civilian courts.

In 321, the emperor issued a decree, that turned Sunday into the "Day of the Lord," an official holiday.

Sylvester had no say in certain important matters. This became clear when a *Desposyni* delegation came to Rome to pay a visit to the bishop. Their spokesman, Joseph, explained to Sylvester that Jerusalem was the center of the Church, not Rome. On top of that, Bishop Clemens of Alexandria had announced that in the second century, James (brother of Jesus), the Nazarene Bishop of Jerusalem, should be seen as "the Lord of the Holy Church" and that he was the "bishop of all bishops." In addition, the bishops of Antioch, Ephesus and Alexandria also had to be a real heritable *Desposyni*. This Jewish-Christian movement had more authority than an invented Roman side-branch originating from Peter. He was simply an apostle of Jesus, not a family member.

Sylvester responded that he was not authorized to repeal the imperial orders of Constantine. By order of the emperor, the teachings of Jesus had been replaced by a doctrine. He thought this was better for the common people and of course, it suited his own purposes much better. In his view, it was he who had liberated the people, not Jesus.

This visit by the *Desposyni* delegation took place in 318; confirmed by the Vatican Archives as well as the historian Eusebius of Caesarea.

The truth of the matter is, however, that Sylvester was never present at important meetings. Not even when the emperor called together all bishops for the first grand ecumenical council in Nicaea in 325. Sylvester had just two priests delegated to this council, which was a wonderful spectacle. About 300 bishops participated, all transported by state carriages. Constantine himself presided over the meeting, but he limited himself to maintaining control. He had based the monopoly of the state on the Christian faith and it was therefore not in his interest that they were divided amongst themselves. The discord had, however, already started in Alexandria and concerned the dogma of the Trinity.

Priest Arius was an ascetic man with grey hair who stood in high regard at the caste of the "Virgins." His vision on the Trinity was, "contrary to the Father and the Spirit, Jesus was no God, but an ordinary human being, who had been born from the union between a man and a woman." This view spread from 313 and many bishops in the Eastern Church shared it. As a result, two factions emerged, the followers of Arius, and the supporters of traditional dogma.

During the council, the majority of bishops gave preference to confirming the traditional dogma. The dogma of the Trinity was incorporated in the "Symbolum Nicaenum," the so-called Nicene Creed.

The priests issued this Creed to their followers and everybody simply had to obey. The text of the Creed is much longer than I describe here, but the core of it is, "I believe in one God, the almighty Father, maker of heaven and earth, and of all things visible and invisible. I believe in one Lord, Jesus Christ, the only-begotten Son of God, born of the Father before all ages. God of God, light of light, true God of true God, begotten, not made."

In fact, humanity was fooled for centuries with this poisonous degradation. Later on, the Church held Constantine in high regard, because he was the cornerstone of the Roman Catholic institution. His Creed became the confession of faith and the basis of dogma that is still in use today.

Despite the fact that "Old School" theologians kept proclaiming that Jesus had been born as a human being, and was not God, but the hereditary Messiah from the line of David, born to his mother Mary, who was *ipso facto* not a virgin.

Constantine was an inventive man who claimed to have seen an illuminated cross. Later on, he even said that Jesus was to blame for the fact that his followers were now in a vulnerable position. Because he had given them freedom, Constantine was their true Savior, not Jesus. He simply pushed the Son of God aside! The emperor claimed the title "Messiah of the Christians" and did all within his power to be regarded as such. Since Jesus was no longer alive, the emperor could even claim the title of "Born again Messiah," as he knew that the Christians awaited the miraculous return of their messiah, Jesus. In this way, Constantine created a new concept, a myth, with his own messianic message.

Emperor Constantine managed to place himself above the relatives of Jesus because the bishops executed his wishes faultlessly. They made sure the new policy was seen as the one and only true religion, given to Constantine by God himself, and claimed that what the *Desposyni* and the Nazarene brotherhood taught was impure, objectionable and heretic. In the end, the Nazarene brotherhood was crushed by the new, official state religion of Rome. This new reality became irreversible.

In his Creed, Constantine merged Jesus and God into one person, so the Son could be identified with the Father. Since the reign of Emperor Augustus, the Roman emperors saw themselves as Gods on Earth and Constantine went the extra mile. He knew better than anyone, that in order to gain even more power and status, he had to make the people believe in something that was out of reach. That is why he made Jesus "Son of God."

We now know this is a distortion of the facts. From old writings, especially the Dead Sea Scrolls, it is apparent that any person who lived according to God's law, was considered a "Son of the Divine Principle." I wonder how Jesus would have felt, if he knew he was the only one to be called "Son of God." I think he would have hated that, for it is the opposite of his teachings and doctrines.

The term "Son of God" is a metaphor stemming from the antique world, used to confirm the bond between God and the human being. The powerful elite of this earth made use of this title and people held them in high esteem in accordance with their rank. The idea of "Son of God" was good in the general sense. This tradition goes far back in history; for instance, to Egypt, where every pharaoh was the son of their god Osiris.

The way people thought in antiquity has been the subject of much research. The Egyptians were familiar with the idea of resurrection and life after death. That was one of the focuses of their religious beliefs. Death brings forth new life, just as spring does in nature. They believed that the deceased had to appear before "the tribunal of the last judgment." He or she would stand in front of the door that led to the hall of the absolute truth, where Osiris sat on his throne.

Osiris lived on earth as a god in human form and taught the people how they should serve and worship God. He brought civilization, but his opponents (evil) killed him. After that, he was resurrected and ascended to heaven, where he would perform the last judgment. The Egyptians believed that Osiris was visible in the sky as the star of Orion. People saw all other stars as the souls of the deceased and Orion guarded them as a good shepherd. This was not the only mythical image that preceded and was adapted in the later concepts of Christianity.

The Greeks adopted this myth from the Egyptians and used it in turn for the divine person Dionysos, who was born from an immaculate virgin, by mediation of the gods. He died in the same way as Osiris, as was also the case with Jesus.

His mother, Olympias, initiated Alexander the Great into the Dionysos cult. She told him that she had also been immaculately conceived and handed him the doctrine that she was a virgin and that he had been conceived by Zeus from mediation of the gods.

For scientists, this aspect was very important. It even supplied conclusive evidence that the story of Jesus was derived from the Egyptian and Old Greek cultures.

Dionysos was literally transformed into "Son of God" and "Saviour of all People." He was depicted as a divine child, resting on his mother's lap, in the same way Jesus was depicted on Mary's lap. And the parallels continue! Dionysos was worshipped with bread and wine, in remembrance of his sacrificial death on a rough wooden stake. He was resurrected and ascended to heaven, just like Osiris.

The link between Egypt and Greece is not strange. The Greek scholar Pythagoras studied in the Egyptian temples for about twenty years. He took his mystical knowledge home to Greece and, instead of introducing a new god, he turned the insignificant Dionysos into a very important one.

Most of the great philosophers in ancient Greece, like Plato and Socrates, were initiated in the cult of Dionysos, which took place mostly in and around Athens. This cult of a dying and resurrected divine human being had thousands of followers.

In the documentary *The Son of God*, broadcast by Discovery Channel in 2003, scientists show that the Church of San Clemente in Rome was built on the foundations of a heathen temple. According to the Roman Church, the heathen ceremonies and rituals that took place there were so appalling to the followers of Jesus, that they erased all their traces. But it is quite remarkable that even in this old temple a savior was worshipped, called Mithras, who, like Jesus, was born from a virgin mother on December 25 and was called "Son of God." He ascended to heaven and would return, in order to judge the living as well as the dead. On the images, heathen priests symbolically celebrate with bread and wine, to honor their savior. The teachings that were attributed to him were as follows, "Whomever does not drink my blood, will not receive salvation!"

Mithras originally came from Persia, but just like Osiris, he had his place in the sky as a star, opposite the astronomical sign of Taurus.

During antiquity, the cult of Mithras was seen as the main competitor of Christianity. Author Tim Freke and historian Professor Keith Hopkins stated: "If Christianity had not been victorious in those days, the whole religious world would now belong to Mithras!"

Constantine incorporated many elements of these old myths in his concepts, which is still the formal basis of Christian thinking.

Jesus was elevated to a divinity and, in the biblical stories, they described him challenging the religious leaders and performing miracles such as changing water into wine. They said he was born from a virgin, died on the cross and rose from the dead at Easter before ascending to heaven. Then the Holy Spirit was poured out over humanity and Jesus' sacrifice brought about the salvation of everybody who adhered to the Christian dogma.

In order to make this recycled fairy tale sound as truthful as possible, they made for Jesus beautiful inscriptions such as, "If you take of his body and drink of the blood of the God-man, you will live and resurrect from the dead."

Therefore, we can conclude that all the images in the myth about Jesus spring from preceding cultures.

The early Christian authors, while stealing ancient myths wholesale, were ordered to somehow obscure all similarities with the ancient cultures' beliefs. In this way, everything was censured and adapted.

The writers that took the story literally, spoke of "imitation by the devil, who had deceived the Egyptian, Greek and Roman people." By putting the blame on the convenient devil, a foundation was made for the idea that he had brought the peoples of the Earth into confusion. The authorities of the Roman Church made sure everything was in accordance with their mythical story.

In the 4th century, Bishop Athanasius of Alexandria wrote about the life of Anthony the Hermit. In his book, he mentions that Anthony battled with the astral forces in his soul. Rome disapproved of this because it was not consistent with their view – Athanasius should have mentioned that Anthony battled with the devil! That would have placed these experiences outside reality, when in fact they had to do with the human struggle of Anthony.

The Church thought it was able to annihilate the truth as a whole and made use of all means that were available to pursue this idea. People became frightened of life after death and priests forced them to obey with threats of eternal damnation and torture in hell and purgatory.

On top of that, certain Greek words were falsely translated. For instance, the Hebrew word *Chahenna* was translated as *hell*, but some research shows that *Chahenna* was simply the name of the dumping ground outside the city walls of Jerusalem, the place where waste burns and lepers live. Even now, a part of that town bears the name *Chahenna*.

The word *virgin* is also mis-translated. Although there is no proof they did this on purpose, this mistake was repeated so often that it makes us think. In the Greek translation (the Septuagint) of the Jewish Bible, they translated "*almah*" (young woman) as virgin. In Hebrew, a virgin is "*bethulah*," a very different word. A virgin and a young woman are not necessarily the same. From the 4th century onward, writers had no choice but to support what Constantine had established. The Christians, who believed this fabrication, literally celebrated their victory by claiming the heathen concepts had become uninteresting and inferior, with the aim to make Constantine's Official State Christianity victorious. On the other hand, people kept their old religious concepts alive and were not prepared to give these up easily.

Constantine arrogantly formed an institutional religion and created a god that was far removed from human beings. At the same time, this caused a social gap between the Christians and the heathens – the inferiors – who in the view of the Christians, were lost anyway.

They called everybody who was not a Christian a *heathen*. The Christians originally used this as a term of abuse, not unlike "clodhopper." They labeled Greek playwrights like Euripides and Sophocles, and the philosophers of the ancient world, as primitive and superstitious farmers. However, when you study these so-called farmers, you will find out that the core of their spiritual thinking contained a rich, mystical philosophy which formed the foundations of the best elements of our Western culture. We cannot dismiss this spirituality as a primitive form of idolatry or dim thinking. On the contrary, the ancient Greek way of thinking was highly evolved. The questions that occupied their minds were "Who am I? What is my purpose? What is the deeper meaning of my existence?" Plato, for instance, saw the human being as a mental prisoner within his physical existence.

In the 5th century, when the bishops of Rome consolidated their position, they decided that Sylvester, a very insignificant bishop in the making of State Christianity, had to be altered, so they invented a legend in which he became an important figure.

They depicted Emperor Constantine as an atrocious persecutor of the Christians. He had become a leper and sought to be cured by the gods. Their advice to him was to bathe himself in the blood of newborn babies, but when he was about to kill a baby, the desperate mother managed to hold him back. During the following night, Peter and Paul appeared to him in a dream. In order to find healing, he had to apply to the Bishop of Rome. *Voila*! Sylvester instructed him in the catechesis, and, after he was immersed in the baptismal water, he came out completely healed.

In his heartfelt gratitude, Constantine lavished the bishop with gifts. He knelt down in front of Sylvester and handed him the imperial tiara and therefore authority over Rome, Italy and the entire West.

This legend has had serious consequences, because it laid the basis for the power of the pope. A few centuries later, this was the cause of one of the greatest swindles in the history of the Church, which will be addressed in a later chapter.

In 598, the Council of Toledo introduced the concept that the Holy Spirit is "from the Father and from the Son." This theological point of discussion divided Christianity into two factions. Because there was no more Western emperor in power at this time, an alternative East-Roman Church developed from its Byzantine base. This Church held to the belief that the Holy Spirit stems "from the Father *through* the Son."

From both viewpoints, they saw Mary no longer as the Mother of God, but as the Mother of the Son. She was the medium through which the Holy Spirit had somehow been passed on.

Nevertheless, a much bigger battle was fought behind the scenes, which was the question whether the Church had to be governed from Rome or Constantinople. Neither of the parties were victorious, and the result was a split into two entirely separate Churches.

In 867, the Vatican broke away from the Eastern Orthodox (Byzantine) Church, which proclaimed that it remained truthful to the apostolic succession. However, the Vatican Council did not agree and therefore Photius, the Patriarch of Constantinople, excommunicated Pope Nicholas I of Rome.

Reading about the different viewpoints and the attitudes of the Churches, it was obvious to me that a huge dispute was being fought within this Catholic stronghold concerning the position of women.

From the beginning, the Church fathers were endemically afraid of women, and in particular of Mary Magdalene. This is why they produced a false document, the Apostolic Church Order, a fictional discussion amongst the apostles. It stated that Mary and Martha were present during the Last Supper, but Jesus did not offer the bread and cup to them, because Mary was laughing. This is why the first apostles decided women could not become priests: they were frivolous, not to be considered seriously! The Church adopted this lie as official dogma and they described Mary Magdalene as unfaithful and disobedient.

In 1977, little had changed, when Pope Paul VI decreed that a woman could not become a priest "because our Lord was a man"!

The Church made diligent use of Paul, portraying him as a man who apparently had an aversion to women. The quotes were chosen very carefully and taken out of context. There is a contradiction in Paul's comments. Sometimes he draws individual attention to his female assistants and praises them for their work, but in other cases, he prohibits them from holding religious office and even attending a service. It is obvious that the Church Fathers chose the fragments that best fitted their interests and ignored the rest. Since the original letters no longer exist, we will never know the literal texts, or whether Paul was even the author.

After the 4th century, the appreciation of women reached a historic nadir, which went on for centuries. During the Middle Ages, Church Fathers Albertus Magnus and Thomas of Aquino adapted the teachings in a most peculiar and even more sanctioned way. They felt that woman was a monstrosity, a failure. *Gnosis*, however, shows us that the female energy is the principle from which the male aspect derives. That is why it was perfectly normal for Jesus to initiate his wife to the highest level. He could not care less how his male disciples felt about this. Peter's envy of his female fellow-thinker runs parallel to how men saw women in later ages.

Albertus Magnus writes at one point that women are less rational than men are. According to him, a woman consists of relatively more fluid. Fluid moves easily, which makes women unstable and curious. He stated that a woman show no loyalty, because when she has sexual intercourse with a man, she wants to be with another man at the same time. Every woman, in his opinion, is a failed man and has a flawed nature, which makes them insecure.

A few ages earlier, Odo, an abbot of Cluny, wrote about women in a scornful way. He said that, if people knew what women are like, just looking at them would cause vomiting. In his view, a woman was a barrel filled with dirt.

"Dignitaries" who were held in high esteem made these statements. The Church even sanctified these "wise" men.

What they did to women in general, through the ages, is truly horrible. The Church's fear of women was so strong, that any who were seen as a threat were condemned as witches, ostracized, tortured, and often burnt on pyres. Shamelessly, the Church Fathers used intimidation, manipulation and narcissism in order to destroy the self-esteem of women.

This is why, as a psychological therapist, I regularly meet women who still suffer this trauma. As long as academics, from their cognitive knowledge, do not want to open up and see that a person goes through several life processes, the suppression of women will never cease. It is not just the burden that a woman carries. In this way, men will never recognize the origin of the engrained viewpoints that they carry with them.

Because of the images I received and the insight I gained, I understood that religion was at the basis of this problem and the world of today is still dealing with it.

Looking at the history of the Church, you find a great discrepancy, not only in the suppression of women, but also in the general field of sexuality.

A clear example of this is celibacy. In the beginning, it was perfectly normal for priests and bishops to be married and to have children.

In the early years of Christianity, sects came into being that banned sexuality. They experienced a dualism between the body and the mind and felt continence was the answer. In the 2nd century an elite group of "virginal adherents" came into being. In the 3rd century, a number of priests tended to cease all sexual intercourse with their wives. In the 4th century, during the Council of Elvira in Spain, the bishops accepted the first legal obligation concerning sexual continence. Bishop Paphnuce found this approach was too rigorous. He felt this would open the door to the loss of moral values, because when nature is constrained it will look for compensation. That is why, in his opinion, marital life is always preferable to secret relationships.

Nevertheless, the trend was set and (to the outside world) bishops, priests and deacons abstained from marital sexual intercourse. As a compensation, the Church gave their wives initiations and appointed them as female bishops, priests and deacons.

Within the Roman Church, it took a long time before the clergymen generally accepted this rule of celibacy. It was not until the 11th century that priests were obliged to send their wives away. In Rome, they went even further: the pope took wives away from their husbands to work for him as slaves in the Lateran Palace!

All other civilizations looked upon the celibacy of the Roman Catholic Church as absurd, exceptional, and often people saw it as suspicious.

Despite the prescribed celibacy, most popes and bishops felt free to be flexible with this rule. They enjoyed sexually extravagant lifestyles in the privacy of their halls of power, apparently unashamed. The Vatican became a meeting place where clergy could come together with male prostitutes and courtesans (high-class prostitutes). The pope and bishops kept these women as their mistresses. Because they moved in the highest circles, they were extremely wealthy and lived lives of great luxury. The women associated themselves with the biblical Mary Magdalene (whom the Church, after all, called a whore) and had themselves painted as a repentant Mary Magdalene. The pope and bishops permitted themselves to make use of these women and, conveniently, this was no problem, as long as both the clergy and the courtesans showed repentance repeatedly about their actions. To donate by a repentant Mary Magdalene, the sinners gained absolution. An "Official" absolution was born, and the sinners adorned lavishly many churches and chapels.

Inevitably, these popes and bishops impregnated their mistresses and, in the 11th century, it was even determined that the papal court could grant hereditary priesthood to their offspring.

Both mistresses of Pope Alexander VI (Rodrigo Borgia) were openly recognized. The famous Vannozza dei Cattanei bore him four children. Among them was the infamous Lucrezia Borgia. Giulia Farnese later replaced Vannozza.

To Pope Julius II (Giuliano della Rovere) one woman at a time was not enough: he had two mistresses simultaneously: Masina and Lucrezia, who bore him three daughters.

The courtesans of the pope enjoyed a special social position and many of them used their position to develop their intellectual and artistic talents, the only avenues open to women in the professional world.

It was the height of hypocrisy, that popes and bishops endorsed monogamous marriage and condemned polygamy, as this (and every other forbidden sexual pastime) is what they practiced.

From the earliest monastic times, there was a constant rivalry and enmity between the monks and the orthodox clergy. The lavish lifestyle of the worldly lords was in sharp contrast with the harsh and ascetic, monastic lifestyle. The monks also showed great discipline in their work, for instance in preserving, assembling and copying historical documents. They would not allow themselves to be influenced by political propaganda or ecclesiastical dogma.

Dogma belongs to a system that forces people to accept things; it does not belong in a system based on choice and free will.

The word "heresy" is derived from the Greek word "hairesis," which means "choice." Therefore, an accusation of heresy equaled a denial of the right to choose. During the time of the Inquisition, it was considered a crime not to obey the regime of Rome and the dogmatic opinions of the bishops.

During the Council of Trullo in 692, they secured the dogma "that Mary had been born as a virgin and conceived of our Lord in an immaculate way," and confirmed "that Mary was forever virgin, even after her Son was born in the flesh."

The whole dogma concerning Mary is, to be frank, sheer lunacy. On the one hand they declared her to be virgin forever, while on the other hand, it is no secret that she had several other children besides Jesus.

In 1622, Pope Gregory XV introduced the *Sacra Congregatio Propaganda Fide* (Sacred Congregation for the Propagation of the Faith), in which he imposed the doctrines as obligatory dogma. The pope founded this "College of Cardinals devoted to the spreading of the faith" with its task to ruthlessly enforce obedience to the Church dogma. Teachers and officially approved historians duly hammered the propaganda home, especially when it was inconsistent with the traditional lore or documented facts.

Not so long ago, the Church still defined several aspects of the Catholic confession of faith as explicit parts of the faith. Before that, they were just implicated.

In 1854, Pope Pius IX decreed that even Mary, daughter of Anna and Joachim, had been conceived without the original "sin." This is the dogma of Mary's Immaculate Conception.

We must differentiate between the dogma of the virginal birth of Jesus and the Immaculate Conception, which refers specifically to the birth of Jesus' mother.

In 1870, during the Vatican Council, they issued this pomposity: "The pope is infallible when he, from his throne, decides about the ecclesiastical dogma and ethics." This ultimate declaration of authority gave a new birth to the inviolability of the pope.

The acceptance of an authority that cannot be mistaken in matters of faith and tradition is dangerous and misleading but, nevertheless, a logical keystone of the structure of the Roman Catholic Church. So far, they have applied the new dogma of infallibility only once, in 1950, and it concerned an aspect of Mariology.

In 1950, Pope Pius XII incorporated the dogma of "Mary's Ascension to Heaven." In 1964, Pope Paul VI proclaimed Mary to be "Mother of the Church."

The papal encyclicals are filled with arrogance and pride.

Take for instance the "*Syllabus Errorum,*" written in 1864. Pope Pius IX writes eighty statements in which he opposes the currents of his time.

> Whoever adheres to the basic thoughts of democracy, whoever advocates freedom of speech, whoever believes in science's claims to truth; *anathema sit* (let him be cursed). [Six years later, the Vatican Council reconfirmed this third element], Whoever claims that the dogma of the Church could ever be enlightened by science in a way that our religion would have to be amended: anathema sit.

This was meant, of course, to uphold the literal interpretation of Genesis against Darwin's revolutionary theory of evolution.

If God does exist, he, she, it, or all of the above, is no human being, but a spiritual, all-embracing energy that is seemingly inexhaustible. This is consistent with science, because life is built up from various forms of energy. That makes complete nonsense of the idea that an inexhaustible force must rest on the seventh day. In Genesis, we read that Adam and Eve were the first human beings, and Cain and Abel were their sons. Genesis 4 adds a third son, called Seth. So, how did Cain, who, after killing Abel over the somewhat trivial matter of whose sacrifice had more favor with God, went to live in the Land of Nod, have intercourse with his wife and beget children? Where did *she* suddenly come from? There is no mention anywhere that Adam and Eve had a daughter.

Even if they had, it would have been incest; and let us be clear: this is not what one expects at the beginning of a religious book. Therefore, it is another nonsensical story.

We have not yet explored the most remarkable piece of text in the Bible, the "Apocalypse of John," or, the "Book of Revelation." Many Christians say these events are still to take place. Let us look at it in detail.

After the apostle John had been exiled to the Greek island Patmos, he wrote this significant text. The Church depicted the Apocalypse as a sinister book dealing with omens and fate and this is how the word "apocalypse" became the symbol of disaster.

It became more and more clear to me that Revelation was in fact a chronological continuation of the Gospels and the Acts of the Apostles. A number of Epistles of Paul and Peter have been placed in between and they are quite dominant, for the simple reason that the Roman Church is based upon their dogma. The Church was not based on Jesus' teachings, contrary to the original "Christianism."

It appears that Revelation has been incorporated into the Bible for a strategic reason. The esoteric content allowed Rome to misinterpret the text from the pulpit. Remember that the common people were incapable of reading the Bible.

This scripture is exactly what it claims to be, a revelation concerning the exile of Mary Magdalene and the imperial persecution of her offspring. John explains, how a woman who wore the crown of Sophia (the crown of twelve stars), fled into the wilderness to get away from the imperial dragon, who wanted to "battle against the rest of her offspring, together with all those who keep God's commandments and stayed truthful to the testimony of Jesus." He mentions the woman was pregnant when she fled: "she was pregnant and cried out in her contractions and labor pains."

Mary Magdalene was indeed pregnant when she and other family members took flight to Gaul. In the Christian tradition of that time, Mary Magdalene represented Sophia (the Greek goddess of wisdom). In the medieval tradition of France and Flanders, Mary Magdalene was called "Notre Dame de Lumière" (Our Lady of the Light) and she was sometimes depicted with a halo of twelve stars.

In his Revelation, John speaks of a great red dragon with seven heads and seven crowns. The Romans had a red dragon on their flag and Rome was referred to as "the City of the Seven Kings," because seven kings had been crowned between 753 and 509 BC, when the republic was founded.

He further relates that the liberation of the *Desposyni*, the offspring of Jesus and Mary Magdalene, meant they could maintain their bloodline, despite the persecutions they had to face. "Because the persecutor of our brothers and sisters, who kept complaining about them to God, has been brought down. They have overcome him, thanks to the blood of the lamb and thanks to their testimonies."

It is clear that Jesus must have died in or before 73, because that year his son, Jesus II Justus, was given the Davidian title: "I, Jesus, sent my angel to announce these things to the communities. I am the descendant of David, his offspring, the radiant Morning Star" (Revelation 22:16).

According to the dogma of the Church, the consecutive weddings in Revelation refer to the wedding of Jesus Christ with the Christian Church. However, there was still no Church when the Apostle John wrote this! The facts were twisted. Here we have a report of an esoteric nature of the family history of the Messiah.

Daughter Tamar (*Damaris* in Greek) married Paul in 53, in Athens. By this marriage, Paul became Jesus' son in law. Church Fathers turned Paul into another character in order to prevent this connection from being known. That is why it is not strange that the later theologians never knew what to make of Paul as the Bible portrayed him. They used to call him "l'enfant terrible" (annoying young person), because his statements and how he is described, do not correspond to the other texts.

The wedding of Jesus Justus is described as the wedding of the Lamb (Revelation 19:7–9). Jesus was referred to as the "Word of God," but besides that, John the Baptist called him the "Lamb of God" (John 1:29). In Revelation *Word* and *Lamb* correspond to Jesus' heirs.

Jesus Justus was forty years old in AD 73. At the wedding meal, his bride was clothed in pure, radiant linen. "Then he said to me: I am a servant just like you and like your brothers and sisters who testify of Jesus. His name was Word of God" (Revelation 19:10-13).

His son, Jesus III, was born in 77 AD and became later "the Alfa and the Omega." This was a Sadducean title of the House of Herod, which was transferred to the House of David in 102, when the power of this dynasty came to an end. He married in 113, with the words: "I am the descendant of David, his offspring, the radiant Morning Star" (Revelation 22:16).

Revelation 16:16 predicts that the great deciding battle between light and darkness (good and evil) will take place in Armageddon (*Har Megiddo*) meaning Mount of Megiddo, an important Palestinian battlefield, where a military fort was located. It guarded the Plain of Jezreel, south of the hills of Galilee.

In the War Scroll (part of the Dead Sea Scrolls), we find a detailed report of the battle that was predicted between the children of the light and the sons of darkness, in the great battle of *Har Megiddo*. On one side were the tribes of Israel and on the other side the Romans and several heathen parties. It was a fierce battle, fought between the light, symbolized by Israel and the darkness of the Roman Empire.

The Roman Church took over and adapted this old concept. The battle of *Har Megiddo* was disengaged from its specific location and adapted to a worldwide scale. Rome took symbolic possession of "the light" for its own use from the day on which Emperor Constantine appointed himself as the leader of Christianity. A decree was issued, saying that the Day of Judgment had not yet arrived, and the bishops approved this decree. The faithful, accepting the revised Principle, were promised entrance to the Heavenly Kingdom. They gave the former hill fort of *Har Megiddo* a supernatural dimension and Armageddon got a frightening connotation. It implied the horrific end of everything – and the only sure way of deliverance was absolute obedience to the Church of Rome. This turned out to be one of the most cunning maneuvers in history, until the truth about Armageddon became known, in 1947.

From this perspective, it became very clear to me, that also in this case the pitcher goes so often to the well that it comes home broken at last. In the Catholic Church, there has always been criticism from within. For instance, the Reformation came about because Luther took a position against the existing dogmas and corrupt practices. In the whole of Church history, we see that if somebody made critical comments, they were regarded as a heretic and silenced by intimidation or pitiless punishment. Even within monasteries and abbeys, opinions were divided.

During the time of Luther, Rome was the religious stock exchange. Simony (selling religious goods and functions) and nepotism (the practice of favoring relatives or friends by giving them positions) were common practice within the churchly hierarchy. When Pope Julius II (called "il terribile" with reason) ruled, the Vatican was the center of sexual extravagance and the whole town was a market selling devotional items.

In Rome, Luther went piously on pilgrimage from one church to the other, earning indulgences everywhere and looking at the relics in awe. However, this complete disorder and blatant spiritual fraud disgusted him, and he openly condemned these practices. He also objected to the "community of saints"; the whole "hocus-pocus," which is now no longer in existence.

Hocus-pocus is an expression that exists in all European countries; derived from the Latin consecration text, Jesus is supposed to have spoken these words during the Last Supper: "*Hoc est corpus* (This is my body)." When spoken quickly it sounds like hocus-pocus and is usually accompanied by the additional words "Pilatus pas," the next words of the Creed. Luther wanted to return to simplicity, using biblical texts as his basis, and be delivered from the Roman Catholic dogmas. Alas, Luther did not realize these texts were not even based on true history.

This is how the Reformation came into existence in 1517 and from which Protestantism developed. It was not only a division, but also the beginning of further disintegration.

In the 18th, 19th and 20th centuries, the Catholic Church lost much of its temporal power. Ruptures appeared in the stronghold of the Church, and it nearly collapsed.

It all started with the French Revolutionaries, who chastised the Church for its lies, superstitions and intrigues, and its unholy league with the French Court. Apart from that, great thinkers like Spinoza, Newton and Voltaire put pressure on the Church by challenging the dogma it proclaimed and brilliantly articulating their doubts. These and others are the founders of The Enlightenment and the freedom of thought that followed.

Let us not forget that Napoleon, for all his many sins against humanity, did break the power of the Church in the end.

From all of this, it is obvious that the Catholic Church has theologically and willfully abused the wealth of Jesus' legacy and nullified it, simply out of self-interest. History shows that people in power have systematically destroyed the inner truth of spiritual revelations. They replace it with an invented religion, with rules and laws and many limitations, designed to perpetuate their dominion; when in fact the most important thing is inner knowledge, an inexhaustible source of great wisdom. This is what Jesus wanted to teach us.

To illustrate this, I quote a text from the Nag Hammadi library, spoken by Jesus.

"Do not impose other regulations than those I explained to you. And do not constitute a law like the legislator, lest you become imprisoned by it."

ABUSE OF POWER & DICTATORSHIP

I n my research, I gradually discovered that the subject of "abuse of power and dictatorship" runs like a common thread through the history of the Church.

Traditionally, the Roman Catholic Church has been an organization in which one man pulls all the strings. Ever since the Congregations of Cardinals was introduced, (the Roman Curia, the administrative office of the pope) this authority has been more widely spread; nevertheless, the Church is still a closed and non-transparent fortress. Its secret service, "*Opus Dei*" has at its disposal great international networks that extend to all layers of society. These networks not only consist of representatives and ambassadors, but also of groups that are less distinguished. The Church never hesitated to engage itself with criminal organizations like the Mafia. In this respect, it bears close resemblance to a worldly dictatorship.

Its position of power was acquired by fraudulent actions, intimidation and threats, even towards the worldly authorities. The Church wanted at a certain moment to increase its status and reached this by blending the name of Jesus with their institute. They fabricated false illustrations and documents with regard to former emperors and popes. For example, it was recorded that Emperor Constantine had received the privilege of calling himself the "Savior of all people," from Jesus himself.

The Christian community started to take the legend of Sylvester seriously. It turned out to be one of the greatest deceptions of the last thousand years of church history. In the eighth century, Pope Zachary had a completely fabricated document made up, allegedly in the handwriting of Emperor Constantine and signed by him: "The Donation of Constantine." In this supposedly four-hundred-year-old document, it was recorded that Jesus himself appointed the pope and assigned him as his replacement on earth.

In this way, the pope built a strong foundation to support all previous illustrations and documents. It was a master forgery, which later popes also used to support their authority and augment their worldly possessions. They completely lost sight of the fact that Jesus had said, "My Kingdom is not of this world."

During the Renaissance, proof was found that The Donation of Constantine was a forgery. In the text, reference is made to the Latin Vulgate of Jerome, who was born in 340, twenty-six years after the document was dated. Besides, it was written in the language of the 8th century.

On the basis of this falsification, the popes started to act like rulers. They even felt that kings were inferior to them, because The Donation of Constantine conveniently stated that God had transferred the power and authority of all dynasties to the pope. This changed the structure of the monarchy.

From then on, the pope crowned the European sovereigns and thus they were not only kings but also servants of the Church, instead of servants of the people. This is the origin of the dictatorship within this Catholic institution, which managed to abuse its power for centuries. The first initiative that Pope Zachary took was to dethrone the Merovingian royal family in France.

The Merovingians were direct descendants of Jesus and his relatives. For 300 years, this dynasty had ruled Gaul. In accordance with their descent, these sovereigns wore their hair long and organized their principality and court according to the example of King Solomon. In 480, King Clovis had made a peace treaty with the Roman Church, but this was rendered useless after 751. The kings of the *Desposyni* dynasties in England and France lived as fathers and servants of the people, and never as their rulers. They were the protectors of the people and their citizens were called sons and daughters of the king. This is in strong contrast to the territorial kingship, a feudal and imperialistic concept that stemmed from the fraudulent document of Pope Zachary. The monarchy of the Merovingians was exclusively dynastic. The hereditary succession was looked upon as an automatic and holy right. The Church had no say in this. Nevertheless, this pure tradition was abolished when Rome took the opportunity to create kings by means of a fake papal law.

The Church thought it could banish the *Desposyni* by persecution and extermination. Yet, the truth could not quite be eradicated.

People were abused on a grand scale, because they were powerless and illiterate. The Church used the military arm of the privileged class, and cleared the road for indoctrination, intimidation and manipulation. The Roman Church is guilty of all three. The faithful believed the threat that, if they did not abide by the dogma, they would spend hundreds or thousands of years in purgatory after death. In severe cases, they would even burn in hell forever.

The Church propagated the story of the fallen angel Lucifer. The devil was born. They burdened humanity with even more fear. However, in fact, they created Satan as a reflection of themselves.

This evil came to be in the ages when Church and State were interwoven. Let us hope that these two powers will never come together again, because history taught us that, when Church and state are not separated, fanaticism reigns and negative forces come forth which we cannot fathom. Even today, we see this result in the endless Middle Eastern conflicts.

In the Early and Late Middle Ages, people had few choices in life. The class structure was rigid. Faith and ethics were established in a system of dogma and regulations, and all opinions that differed were considered to be heretic. A heretic was by definition an enemy of the Church. Because Church and State were one, the religious heretic was also an enemy of society.

Disobedience had great consequences; so many people simply did as was expected of them. By this fear, we forget to listen to our inner voice and thereby be ourselves. The churchly institute was dictatorial and did not shy away from the use of violence. Its authorities were arrogant and hypocritical. When somebody refused to accept the faith and subject themselves to the ecclesiastical dogma, the consequence was torture, often ending in death.

They practiced this abuse of power for over a thousand years. Despite the fact that the Roman Church no longer has any worldly power, these conservative forces are still very much present. Simply look at the fact that the authorities in Rome still want to determine how people should deal with their sexuality.

The Roman Catholic Church still decides, be it from the background, how over a billion people think about life and death. The pope and bishops still raise their moralizing finger when confronted with active or passive euthanasia. I have vivid memories of a newspaper article in 2002, in which a Dutch bishop made a statement about active euthanasia. He literally said, "When somebody chooses this form, he cannot receive the sacrament of the ill and he can also not be buried with official Catholic rituals. This is only possible when the priest in office is not informed." In other words, let us pretend we did not notice! This hypocritical uttering is a typical example of Catholic obscurity and manipulation.

This Church itself committed torture, rape and murder. Popes were guilty of promoting genocide and discrimination against large groups of native people around the world; but kept silent about their own polygamy and other rancid excesses. This Church should keep quiet, admit its sins, and give up all forms of authority.

Even during the last few centuries, those who resisted were ruined completely. Priests personally took care of this. My mother told me that during her youth everybody followed Church orders without independent thinking. Whether you were a manager, teacher, laborer or mayor, it made no difference; it was common practice. When somebody protested, punishment by shame and ostracism immediately followed and in such a way, that the sinner could serve as an example to others. In these cases, it was very clear to people, the Church did not tolerate this kind of behavior and when you did it anyway, it only led to your own demise. That was a bleak prospect and therefore people held themselves strict to the rules. In the 20th century, the church was critical of regimes that hid and denied their criminal behavior, while at the same time making deals with men like Hitler and Mussolini. The Church itself had sown the seeds and now they forgot to organize their own affairs.

The Church has always abused human emotions and spread fear, thus taking away people's free choice. Children were infected in their early stage of development and, in a subtle way, emotionally driven in one direction. I only have to recall my own youth, and how I was indoctrinated by people who said things like, "I bet you will become a priest as well, right? Oh, your parents will be so proud!"

Apart from this, children were sexually abused for many decades. Just look at the recent disclosures on this subject. It's a good thing that the Dutch Investigative Committee Deetman was instituted in order to look into this, though this in itself is not enough. Seeing how the Church, in this case a bishop, apologized on a television show, is food for thought. The apology was spoken deliberately, in a cold and businesslike manner, without any form of compassion or empathy for the victims. No emotion was expressed, which is astonishing considering that tens of thousands of people have fallen victim to abuse and rape within the Church.

Only one conclusion is fitting: this churchly institute has caused so much misery, sorrow and pain, that it has lost its right to speak.

THE CRUSADES

The crusades took place between 1095 and 1271. They were military enterprises, undertaken by the popes that ruled during this period. The declared purpose of these crusades was to liberate the Holy Land from the Muslims, but they degenerated into huge massacres and depredations that were unequalled. Time and again, the crusades left a trail of blood and destruction in Europe and the Middle East. Wherever the crusades arrived, people were forced to convert to the one true religion. Those that refused were slaughtered by "Holy Warriors" commissioned by the pope in Rome.

The participants were mostly noblemen and knights, who joined up with their own interests at heart. For instance, with the purpose of acquiring land or money in exchange. Many had lost their land because of redistribution, as a consequence of the feudal system. There was the added benefit of automatic forgiveness for all their sins. Traders also went along, because they were interested in developing trade between the Middle East and Western Europe.

There was great poverty and discontent in Europe, causing enormous social problems. The people were desperate and furious because of the absurd wealth of the pope and the Holy Church. Because the churchly authorities were afraid there would be derailment and aggression, peasants, vandals, mercenaries who plagued the land with looting, rape and murderer were also allowed to join in. They were given a free hand to rob, kill and plunder somewhere else; and so, there was no shortage of volunteers. This way they could relieve their own poverty and give full vent to their aggression; moreover it solved a big problem for the popes and kings.

The motives of the Church were not just to liberate Palestine and Jerusalem, but also to extend its power to the east.

Inciting the crusades lent the pope a certain authority in relation to the emperor, because it was unprecedented for a religious leader to incite organized warfare. Behind this was a dispute of competence between pope and emperor, which led to the Investiture Controversy.

During the Council of Clermont (November 26, 1095) Pope Urban II incited the first crusade. Byzantine Emperor Alexius I had asked for military assistance against the Seljuk Turks. The pope consented, because his first goal was to liberate the Holy Land from the Muslims, supposedly in order to make Jerusalem a safe place for Christians. Here was a chance for adventure, wealth, and forgiveness for all your sins, even the sins you commit while on crusade. Men reacted to this unleashing of greed and religious fanaticism with great enthusiasm!

Altogether, there were nine crusades. The last one ended in 1272. The horrible massacres that took place during these so-called Holy Wars, would now be judged as crimes against humanity. Later on, Romanticism embraced and glorified this churchly military endeavor. In this way, the crime and genocide instigated by the Roman Catholic Church was downplayed and pushed into the background.

THE ORDER OF THE KNIGHTS TEMPLAR

The Order of the Knights Templar consisted of knights who had joined forces in order to protect pilgrims in the Holy Land. In 1120, they laid down the monk's vow for the Archbishop of Jerusalem and swore to protect the holy sites. They were accommodated in a wing of the palace of King Baudouin II, that bordered the former Al-Aqsa Mosque. Before long, they had the whole Temple Mountain at their disposal. On this hill, King Solomon had built his temple, around 1000 BC. But thereof was nothing more to be found, after it was destroyed in 70 CE by the Roman empire. A part of the treasure of Jerusalem had been hidden before the invasion by Nebuchadnezzar of Babylon in 586 BC; another part was hidden in the 1st century, during the Jewish Rebellion against the Roman occupation.

Almost immediately after their profession, the group started to call itself the "Order of the Temple." Their patron was Bernard of Clairvaux, Church Pastor and founder of the Cistercian Order. He appointed Hugh de Payens as Grand Master of the Knights Templar. During the famous Council of Troyes in 1129, Bernard recorded the rules and regulations of the order. He set the requirement that they live in complete obedience to the teachings of Jesus and Mary Magdalene, and that they would protect those of the *Desposyni* who were still alive.

The Temple Order was independent of the Church and monarchy. It fell under the personal authority of the Pope of Rome. The Knights Templar could ordain their own priests and were exempted from churchly taxes. The regular clergy had a hard time accepting the Knights' privileged position, even though other monastic orders knew similar privileges.

The Temple Order fought in the Holy Wars against Islam, protected the pilgrims and safeguarded the routes along which they travelled to the Holy Land. Despite the fact that they were a monk order, the Knights Templar were primarily military. They saw themselves as the Christ's Militia. They were allowed to kill Muslims, but any who killed a Christian were evicted from the order. The Knights Templar were infamous for their religious fanaticism and military character. They were fierce fighters against the enemies of their faith. On the other hand, they were also a traditional monastic order. They had to renounce worldly matters, in order to serve God and save their souls. They knew the common monk's vows of poverty, chastity and obedience. In their daily lives, the monks were required to pray, to do penance and to share with the poor. They had their meals in communal halls, in complete silence, listening to someone reading from the Bible. The crown of their heads was shaved and they grew beards. The knights wore a white shirt and the common soldiers a brown or black shirt. On the front was embroidered the famous Templar's Red Cross, the symbol of Christ's suffering. During the chapter meetings, all who were present had to confess their sins. The members were absolutely forbidden to own money or goods. Gambling and excessive drinking were prohibited, and the company of women was not allowed.

The Order needed men and means. For this reason, the first Grand Master made a propaganda tour through Europe and managed to interest many royal families and rich noblemen in the movement.

The order became very rich, very fast. They owned many large estates in the Kingdom of Jerusalem and in Europe. When noblemen joined the order, they abided by the vow of poverty and donated all of their worldly possessions to the order. On top of that, the order was exempted from paying taxes. Because of this, but also because, according to popular belief, they were in possession of the treasures of Solomon that they had retrieved, the Knights Templar became the most successful financial organization in history. They served as financial advisors and bankers of monarchies in all of Europe. The Temple Order grew to be the most powerful and prestigious brotherhood of the Middle Ages.

During the building of the basilica of La Sainte Baume (The Holy Balm) in France, a church devoted to Mary Magdalene, Pope Boniface VIII entrusted the relics of Mary Magdalene to the Knights Templar. He did this because of their high status and capacity to safeguard things. King Philip IV ("the Fair") was jealous and furious about this, more so because he owed the Temple Order a fortune in loans. He also feared their political and esoteric power, which far exceeded his own. He was convinced they had brought the treasures of Solomon, as well as the Ark of the Covenant, from Jerusalem to France. He started a hate campaign against the Knights Templar and Pope Boniface.

The test for young knights consisted of preparing them for possible capture by the Muslims. During this test they had to worship an idol in the form of a cat, called Baphomet. This Knights Templar "jest" was seen as heresy by their enemies. Anyway, Baphomet is a code that was used quite often by the Knights Templar, and it could be translated as *Sophia*, signifying the goddess of wisdom, Mary Magdalene. The Knights Templar felt very strongly about wisdom, so this "jest" must have had a deeper meaning.

During the crusades there were also peaceful intervals, in which contact was made with the Arab population. Because of this contact, the

Knights Templar became familiar with an art of living, philosophy and science that was unknown in Europe. They outgrew their European contemporaries.

The Knights Templar were mostly interested in the production of pure gold, because its properties of centrifugal force were important in the building of the French Gothic cathedrals. Philip IV admired their scientific knowledge.

The one-atomic gold powder was called the "philosopher's stone" by chemical analysts like Nicolas Flamel and it was used in the fabrication of the dazzling stained glass windows which were designed by Persian philosophers of the school of Omar Khayyám. Nicolas claimed that in order to make glass following their special procedure, they made use of the *Spiritus Mundi*, the cosmic breath of the universe.

In the sixteenth century, the alchemist Sancelrien Tourangeau wrote that "our stone grants all kinds of inner colors to the glass." This specific Cistercian Templar's glass was used for the windows of the Sainte-Chapelle in Paris, as well as the churches of Saint-Gatien and Saint-Martin in Tours.

The Knights Templar called this part of their activities "Ormus." A few decades ago, this science was rediscovered and the specific gold powder was called "Ormes." The Knights Templar found the alluvial gold they needed for the production of the exotic Ormus material in Bézu (Languedoc, south-eastern France). Surrounding Bézu were old mines, rich in gold close to the surface. Bertrand de Blanchefort was the owner of this country estate. Later on, he became a Grand Master of the Knights Templar.

From 1296, the activities were concentrated in one main building; the workshop in the nearby Campagne-sur-Aude. Knights were imported from Aragon in order to constantly watch the building from observation posts. The area was under the authority of the Spanish King of Aragon. King Philip suspected that the treasures, as well as the Ark of the Covenant and the relics of Mary Magdalene, were kept there. However, since the Knights Templar were autonomous within their own region and only had to bow down to the pope, he could not attack Bézu directly. That is why he wanted a pope whom he could manipulate, to grant him the necessary freedom.

King Philip had Boniface VIII killed, and his successor, Benedict XI, was poisoned by Philip's chancellor, Guillaume de Nogaret. He was, in 1305, replaced by the king's own candidate, Bertrand de Got, Archbishop

ABUSE OF POWER & DICTATORSHIP

of Bordeaux, who became Pope Clemens V. Philip had complete control over the new pope and, in this way, he could isolate the brotherhood in Bézu, so they could get no one's support anymore. Then, his accomplices struck on Friday October 13th, 1307.

This is the origin of the popular superstition that Friday the 13th, is an ill omened day!

But the king underestimated the secret network of the Knights Templar. The chaplain of La Buzadière was informed of the intentions of Philip the Fair and seven knights received orders to convey the news to the key locations of the order, including Paris, Saint-Malo and Bézu.

The larger part of the treasure was hidden in the vaults of their Chapter Hall in Paris – the background for the famous painting of 1147 of the Knights Templar with the Ark of the Covenant. It is now exhibited in the Château de Versailles. He had the treasure of Paris transported by a fleet of galleys, from La Rochelle to Scotland and Portugal.

When Philip's men arrived in Bézu, they found it empty and abandoned. But the messengers that were sent to inform the Knights Templar of Philip's attack often came too late. All over France, many were arrested.

The king had drawn up a list of allegations against the Order, the main accusation being heresy. The Knights were questioned, tortured, imprisoned and some were burnt alive. People were bribed or forced to testify against them. Many of them disappeared without a trace.

One claim was that the Knights owned a human skull which they revered in a ceremony. Guillaume de Nogaret had the Knights Templar questioned with the use of torture, but nevertheless, Philip did not find out where the skull of Mary Magdalene was kept. On March 18, 1314, the last Grand Master, Jacques de Molay, died on a pyre in Paris. He had always kept silent during his trial. The accusations of heresy, homosexuality and adoration of Baphomet were unprecedented in those days. While on the pyre, De Molay cursed the king as well as the pope. Both died within a year.

Philip the Fair had still not managed to completely eradicate the Knights Templar. After the order was discontinued, many members, having fled with their possessions, were taken in by the Knights Hospitaller. They changed their name to *Knights of Christ*.

The Order of Hospitallers was known for taking care of sick pilgrims in Jerusalem. The archives of the Knights Templar had been lost and the members were under the strict obligation not to talk to others about the Templar Order. This kind of secrecy was quite common for brotherhoods.

Among Freemasons and lovers of esoteric knowledge, the story goes that the Order of the Knights Templar remained secretly in existence for centuries. In some books one can read that there are, up to the 20th century, functioning Grand Masters of the Order.

Even now, there is the question of great treasures that were hidden in the surroundings of Bézu by the Knights Templar. Bérenger Saunière, the village priest of Rennes-le-Château, discovered this. More about this later.

In 2001 Professor Barbara Frale found by accident the "Chinon Parchment" in the Vatican Secret Archives. This document dates from 1308-1314 but was found in the archive dedicated to the 17th century. It gives a description of the interrogations of 79 Knights Templar, held in the castle of Chinon. It also contains notes made by Pope Clemens V, directed at Bishop Jacques Fournier, who later became Pope Benedict XII. They show that in 1314, Clemens acquitted the Knights Templar of heresy, lent them papal absolution and even asked for their forgiveness. He had disbanded the Temple Order only under political pressure by King Philip IV. On October 25, 2007, the Vatican published the book *Processus contra Templarios* and declared the Knights Templar no longer to be heretics. This publication was based on the "Chinon Parchment."

In 2008, descendants of the Knights Templar in Spain filed a law suit against Pope Benedict XVI, in order to restore the good name of the Temple Order.

The Murder of the Albigensians

Despite the fact that in the 8th century, the Merovingian sovereigns had been dethroned by the pope in an illegal and aggressive manner, the heritage of the *Desposyni* was saved.

Many of these Merovingians went into hiding and by reunification in the Languedoc they were able to hold on. They called themselves the Albigensians and turned this area into the most prosperous region of Western Europe. Later, they were referred to as Cathars, because the pope accused them of heresy. They abided by the Gnostic teaching of Jesus and not by the Church dogma.

In those days, the city of Albi was an important center. In the old language of Provence, the word *albi* also referred to a female fairy. Originally, this word came from the Old Testament and was a title for the head of a Royal family (elef). The name *albi* was a tribute to the royal heritage of the Davidian dynasty.

The word Cathar literally means "the pure one." They were very spiritual people and believed that an individual is a pure spirit that transcends the physical. Contrary to the greedy practices of Rome, they were open and transparent in their convictions. But the fear of the Pope for the Cathars was caused by something much more threatening. They were the guardians of a great treasure, that had to do with an esoteric wisdom, called *Sapientia*, which eclipsed Roman Christianity. Jesus had left this wisdom in the care of Mary Magdalene and their offspring. They were of course the royal heirs of Jesus and posed a great threat to the Pope of Rome. They were living proof that the dogma of the Roman Catholic Church was a tissue of half-truths, fantasies and outright lies.

Contrary to the bigotry of the Roman Church and popular hatred, the Cathars took a tolerant stance towards the Jewish and Muslim cultures. Moreover, they maintained equality of the sexes. These were the reasons they were condemned by the Catholic Inquisition. They were also accused of blasphemy and perversion. These false accusations were contradicted by witnesses who later testified to the harmonious way the Cathars lived together, to their charity and their unbending devotion to the teachings of Jesus.

They believed in God and had an exemplary society with good social care, like schools for the poor and hospitals. They lived in peace with others of different faith. They let everybody share in their prosperity and never imposed their convictions or views on anyone. They were non-conformist, preaching without permit, and had no need for specially appointed priests or richly adorned churches. Bernard of Clairvaux, a church teacher as well as a dreaded opponent of the pope, openly declared that no preaching was as Christian as theirs, and that their moral principles were pure.

At this moment the area belongs to France, but in those days, it was an independent state that fell under the dominion of the Count of Toulouse with political connections to Spain. The Albigensian society was tolerant and cosmopolitan, contrary to the rest of Western Europe. It was the center of poetry, troubadours and the courtly love culture. They taught classical languages, literature, philosophy and mathematics. The area was prosperous and economically stable, but that came to a truly apocalyptic end beginning in 1209.

France became divided, because in the north and central areas of the country was great need. King Philip II, together with the nobility, looked suspiciously towards the Albigensians and their jealousy changed to hatred against those prosperous people in the south.

In 1208, the Cathars were handed a severe warning by Pope Innocent III for their supposed unchristian behavior. The Pope and the King of France joined forces because both had an interest in eliminating the Cathars. They were looking for an opportunity to influence public opinion in their interest and they were successful. One of the Pope's representatives in the Languedoc, Pierre de Castelnau, was killed by anti-Church rebels. Rome did not hesitate to seize the opportunity to blame the Cathars. In 1209, a papal army of 30,000 men, headed by Simon de Montfort, departed to the Cathar region. The fighters were disguised as Knights of the Cross and had a holy mission: to eliminate the Albigensian community. It is therefore called the "Albigensian Crusade."

The massacres lasted, all together, for 35 years and many tens of thousands of Cathars were killed. There was one day in which 20,000 people were burned alive, when the town of Béziers was laid in ashes. According to the Pope, it was no problem that orthodox Catholic citizens were also within the town walls during the burning, because "in the afterlife the Lord would recognize His own people." Standing before the gates of heaven, the Catholics would be separated from the heretics! (*Kill 'em all and let God sort 'em out*).

On March 16, 1244, the holy mission reached its climax in a horrendous massacre. The great and historic Montségur, the last fortress of the Cathars that remained standing, fell after a siege of ten months. The Cathars, to the end, bravely refused to repent – and this is why more than two hundred hostages were burned alive on the final pyre.

The Church attempted to find the secret documents and treasures of the Cathars, but they were taken to safety by some who managed to escape from the fortress. After the fall of Montségur, the Gnostic teaching openly disappeared from our culture.

Seen from a historical perspective, this massacre by the Roman Church is completely incomprehensible, because the Cathars formed no threat. The fact that they were linked to a very special old science was not new. After all, Guilhèm of Toulouse had founded his Jewish Academy 400 years before. But Innocent III and his bishops feared that the *Desposyni* among them would expose and overthrow the church dogma, as this was not based on any real foundation. That's why this fanatical and criminal regime saw only one solution: the order to "kill all Cathars and their supporters." This sentence also applied to those who sympathized with the Cathars, and they were many. With this tyrannical and bloodthirsty action, Pope Innocent III gave a strong impetus to the recently organized Inquisition.

THE INQUISITION

The Churchly Inquisition (the Holy Office), was set up in 1147 during the Council of Reims. This was the first meeting between the Pope and his bishops, specifically to make plans for an organized extinction of heresies (any independent thought not abiding by the ecclesiastical dogma).

In 1184, the Synod of Verona followed, in which Pope Lucius III, in accordance with Emperor Frederic II of Italy, evoked the worldly powers to take measures against the heresies, which were at the time widespread in Europe.

It is important to note that most who were labeled as heretics were striving to regain the true Christianity of the time of the apostles and the early Church. This is an understandable desire, seen from a viewpoint of confrontation with the Roman Church, which by her riches and her greed for worldly power had little to do with what the New Testament said about what it means to be a Christian.

Manual laborers protested against the wealth and lifestyle of the clergy (those holding clerical office), because they longed for a Church that would follow apostolic standards. This longing was seen only as dangerous criticism by the Church.

The Inquisition was a court of justice within the Roman Catholic Church, responsible for the tracing and punishing of heretics. Inquisition is the Latin word for "investigation." This court investigated, formulated the verdict and condemned the heretics.

The Inquisition is often falsely compared to the Council of Troubles, a specialized court that was not established by the Roman Church in 1567, but by the Duke of Alva. It was commissioned by the Spanish King, and was only active in the Netherlands, especially against the Protestants.

In 1211, Simon de Montfort called together the "parliament" in Pamiers. He was the worldly leader of the crusade against the Cathars. A problem had arisen because the papal legate, the Cistercian Arnaud Amaury, was supposed to have said: "Although I wish for the death of the enemies of Christ, as a monk and priest, I cannot kill them."

A solution was sought and found: the Churchly Inquisition would point out the heretics and dictate an appropriate punishment, which worldly powers would execute. A churlish way to pretend their hands were clean of blood. There were a number of other rules laid down, the most influential being the one that said monks and priests, who were assigned to implement the Inquisition on behalf of the Church, were placed in a position above that of the worldly power. Therefore, they too did not have to account for their actions.

With the Rules of Pamiers, the Inquisition was for the first time formally institutionalized on a diocesan level. The cooperation of Church and State was secured and the Inquisition could regionally take on the form of a systematic persecution of all opposing forces.

In several papal decrees, different aspects of the application of this method were filled in. Only after the collection of decrees of Pope Gregory IX in 1234, was there a more or less uniform and consistent issuing of rules in this field.

In 1232, Gregory gave orders to the new Dominican Order, to take upon itself the task of the Inquisition. This is how the Inquisition was formally acknowledged and installed. The Pope also charged, in 1237, the Franciscan Order with the Inquisition.

In 1243, Pope Innocent IV decided that torture was allowed when interrogating the suspects, with the aim of forcing them to confess.

From this point on, the Inquisition, under direct supervision of the Pope, became an inviolable, criminally-empowered tyranny over people who had no way of defending themselves. A power, not only of the Church in relation to the people, but also within the Church itself. This can be concluded from the following.

To the monks, the ideal of poverty, as practiced by the sanctified Francis of Assisi, was the only road to God. But the Spirituals (followers of Francis) were condemned in great numbers as heretics and punished accordingly. Poverty, indeed! Fine for peasants and minor priests, but the Church Fathers had bigger (and tastier) fish to fry.

The way the Church proceeded was often very subtle. A delegation of inquisitors would arrive in a village and the priest would be asked to assemble the whole community in the church. Everybody would come, because it would be very suspicious not to attend. Then the inquisitors would speak to those present and exhort them to repent their sins.

Confessions were heard, and small heretical shortcomings would be forgiven, on condition that the person repented and was prepared to denounce two other heretics. This caused a chain reaction of allegations. This and other techniques were not lost on more modern police states.

The severe cases were marked down on a list and a long waiting period was given between summons and presentation. The idea behind this was to give the suspect ample time to think about the questions they would ask him. Even during questioning, the suspected recusant was kept in the dark as to what he was accused with, meaning that he had no idea what he was up against. After a long interrogation that left the suspect terrified and totally confused, he was charged with some form of heretical behavior. Often it was then too late, and the defendant would be confronted with his own earlier statements.

These processes were unfair and unworthy, because:

> It was impossible for the accused to confront the prosecutor. The charge could be given anonymously and if there was no charge it could simply be made up.Prosecutor and judge were often one and the same person; the judge could investigate and formulate the charge himself. The suspect could be detained indefinitely until the prosecution was ready to proceed.The accused did not have the right to be informed of the charge until he or she was already, for all intents and purposes, condemned.Torture was allowed (practically compulsory) during interrogation and, from 1570, the safeguards that were initially incorporated in the system were abolished.The suspect was not allowed an attorney.The suspect could not call on witnesses.

> The suspect could not interrogate witnesses for the prosecution. From 1590, an accusation coming from the people was no longer needed; it was not even necessary to prove anything in a legal sense. Appealing to a higher court was impossible.

The coercion during these trials was not meekly applied. Confessions were enforced by means of threats and torture. People were tied and racked, burned with red hot pokers, hung in agonizing positions – whatever the interrogator's fertile imagination could conceive. After the victim had confessed to whatever insane fantasy they had cooked up, if he repented he was decapitated or hanged; if not, he was sentenced to burn on the pyre at an always-popular Auto-da-Fé. But, whether he died during the interrogation or after the conviction was of no concern to the inquisitors, because the result was the same for them: The Church had been liberated from another heretic.

After 1400, when the French and Italian Inquisition had lost their strength, the violence raged again in Spain. The Spanish Inquisition was largely focused on Jews and Muslims, but gradually spread out over all of Europe. The character was the same and it was just as harsh. The screaming and the flames lasted until 1834.

After 1520, absolutist sovereigns tried to centralize the legislation in a way that suited their purposes. The traditional jurisdiction, in which a person was accused and defended, was replaced by the Inquisition. This dominant form of jurisdiction was, under the influence of the Church, initiated in most of Europe, with England the only exception.

THE PERSECUTION OF WITCHES

In times when superstition was prominent, the churchly authorities feared the intuitive side of women, because they could see through their intrigue and other falsehoods. Women engaged in all kinds of "heathen rituals," such as traditional healing, and they posed a great threat to the male rulers' hegemony.

They were considered inferior, but because Dominic (the founder and religious leader of the Dominican Order of friars) was opposed to women, they became the focus of the inquisitors. After 1380, women were actively persecuted, because, according to the Inquisition, they had supernatural powers at their disposal. This is why they were called witches.

The inquisitors abused their position of power on a grand scale and behaved like barbarians. Occasionally, an inquisitor would visit the accused women in the dungeons, seek one out and then take her away for interrogation. With a great show of power and under threat, she would then be sexually abused by this inquisitor. After that, he would have her tortured and killed, because this malicious woman had obviously tried to seduce him, a monk.

It may be understandable that a real criminal, such as a violent killer, would receive a death sentence. But to condemn a woman to death for nothing but *being* a woman, is disgusting and horrendous!

In many ways, these battles were fought simply to keep women subdued and to control their imaginary powers of corruption. Churchly and governmental rules, like the introduction of mandatory marriage, were supposed to contribute, but, like any rule which directly opposes human nature, did not work out.

This amendment of law coincided with the high degree of fear people had of sin, hell and the devil. As from 1450, women who did not live a life of chastity, and obedience to the authority of their husbands, were accused of being witches who had made a pact with the devil. They were accused of having voluntary sex with the devil on Witches' Sabbath. During the interrogations, under the most atrocious methods of torture, women were forced to name other participants in the Witches Sabbath; these women were arrested as well and went through the same ordeal. And so, from 1580 onwards, the infamous mass trials came into being, during which tens of thousands of women were killed. The Inquisition placed a severe strain on humanity.

On May 13, 2000, in a public admittance, Pope John Paul II asked forgiveness for the mistakes the Catholic brothers and sisters had made in the past. By this historical gesture, the Roman Catholic Church wished to enter the 3rd millennium with a clean sheet.

People criticized this "Mea Culpa," because forgiveness was asked solely for acts committed by individual believers, not for the malignant policies implemented by several popes and other churchly authorities, which made this cultural genocide possible. Even during World War II, the Catholic Church did not have clean hands. Just remember the dubious role of Pope Pius XII, with regard to extradition of Jews, socialists, gypsies, homosexuals, et alia, to the Nazis' new and improved version of Hell on earth. The Catholic Church did not oppose the mass murder of Jews and justified it by issuing the old favorite canard that they were guilty of the death of their Jesus Christ.

This Church has been a source of evil from the start. It has been instrumental in corruption, arrogance and abuse of power within its own organization and even more so in society as a whole. Throughout the centuries it has left its mark upon all of humanity.

It is absurd that this institution is still able to keep its balance and does not have to answer for all its crimes. In our Dutch democracy, ministers are called to account by parliament and even heads of state are liable when they are found guilty of genocide or overriding human rights. Especially because of this, it is unbelievable that Vatican City, a miniature state that does not amount to much, is still being shielded by fanatical Christian governments and exempted from all democratic responsibilities.

It is easy to imagine why a virtuous man like the Patriarch of Venice, Pope John Paul I, wanted to end the impure practices that went on within Vatican City. Alas, his pontificate did not last very long, because he was eliminated by his opponents. But whether it concerns John Paul I, or anyone else, like the current Pope Francis, true honesty, justice, and atonement will not be tolerated within the closed circuit of the Church.

The history of papacy has grown into a treacherous tumor within this Church, filled with pus from its own dark past. There has even been a period which is called "the night" of the Roman Catholic Church.

Charity is at the core of the Christian dogma, but instead of practicing it, the clergy only preached it.

Papal Disorder

Even though I was aware of the fact that the Roman Catholic Church has a history of disorder and horror, I was still amazed by what I found in *The True Story of the Popes*. It made the hairs stand up on the back of my neck.

I have no intention of making a list of all popes of the past. There have only been a few virtuous and intellectual popes. The overwhelming majority were power-hungry fanatics, mostly bent on enriching themselves and their families. Many popes lived licentious lives. Some were perverted, others were psychotic and paranoid by nature.

By showing some bizarre examples, I would like to acquaint the reader with some of the personalities that were hidden behind the title, "His Holiness the Pope."

From the beginning, there was a power struggle about the bishops' choice of Rome, especially after Constantine had applied some structure. The inhabitants of Rome had been given the right to choose their new bishop. The rich and noble families had interest to get their candidate elected, so they opposed one another and thereby no stone was left unturned. Bribery, threats and even murder were the order of the day.

It did happen that the chosen candidate was not accepted by the people. Then this bishop would be expelled or imprisoned.

There were also cases where the chosen one was not even a priest. He would then receive the necessary ordinations in no time, before he was installed.

After the 8th century, the pontificate became more and more important and desirable, because the bishops had acquired worldly power thanks to the "Donation of Constantine."

Within the Eastern Church, the bishops made use of the title "Pope" when referring to colleagues. Later on, this use of the term was adopted by Archdeacon Leo, who became Bishop of Rome in 440. He believed that he had the sole right to the title. After all, from the beginning, the Church had propagated the lie that Peter was tied to the episcopal throne of Rome.

His successor, Pope Gelasius (492-496), usurped all power and placed himself on the throne like a god. He rejected any imperial interference and informed the emperor in a letter:

> Illustrious Emperor, there are two sorts of power which rule the world: the holy authority of bishops and the authority of kings. The authority of bishops is superior to that of kings because bishops have to give account before the divine court for all people, even for kings. Your pious Majesty will decide henceforth, that nobody will ever, and under any human pretext, resist the unique function of the one that was placed above all others, following Christ's orders, and is seen as the leader by the Holy Church. Human audacity can attack what is based on this firm divine right, but wherever the attack might come from, this legitimacy cannot be overruled.

In his self-satisfaction, he took care that the heathen festivity of Lupercalia was replaced by the Christian celebration of Candlemas.

Felix IV, the son of a priest, became pope in 526. He fell ill soon after. He knew his days were numbered and appointed Archdeacon Boniface as his successor. The clergy did not agree with this and appointed Dioscorus as successor, shortly before the death of Felix. Boniface, of course, did not agree with *this*, and made sure the newly chosen pope would not survive. Three weeks later, Dioscorus died.

The new pope, Boniface II, pronounced "anathema" upon the deceased pope and the priests who chose him. He also obligated these priests to sign the condemnation of Dioscorus.

Silverius was the son of Pope Hormisdas and was consecrated as pope in 536. Empress Theodora, in Constantinople, felt that this pope had to disappear and that one of her protégés, Vigilius, had to be the new pope. She hatched a plan and managed to bribe Antonina, wife of the Byzantine general Belisarius. In March of 537, Pope Silverius fell victim to Antonina and husband Belisarius, who locked the Pope in a small room. The clergy was informed that Silverius had admitted he was guilty of treason. On March 19th, Vigilius became the new pope.

Emperor Justinian filed a lawsuit at the request of the Bishop of Lycia. This bishop was convinced of Silverius' innocence. But Vigilius devised a ruse by asking permission from the emperor to take the imprisoned pope under his protection. Silverius was handed over to his arch-rival, who banished him to the island of Sponza. There, Pope Silverius gave up his office "voluntarily" in favor of Vigilius, who promptly had his predecessor starved to death.

Gregory was a brilliant lawyer and an important magistrate of Rome. He was the great- grandson of Pope Felix III and when his father died he inherited estates all over Italy. He sold them all and founded a Benedictine monastery on Sicily, to which he retreated. Pope Pelagius II appointed him as Deacon and arranged for him to be his representative at the imperial court in Byzantine. Emperor Maurice wanted him to be the successor. Gregory refused and tried to flee. Against his will, he was forced to accept the office of pope in 590. Despite everything, this pope enjoyed enormous popularity and went into history as Gregory the Great.

His successor Sabinianus was consecrated in 604. He was very jealous of his predecessor's popularity and accused him of having squandered Church possessions. However, Sabinianus himself sold grain belonging to the Church at extortionate prices to the famished citizens of Rome.

After a few Greek and Syrian popes, the power struggle between Rome and Byzantium flared up again. Bishop Gregory was inaugurated as pope and Emperor Leo III made plans for his assassination. But the attempt was thwarted because the pope had supporters from several sides. Pope Gregory II focused on the German states and urged the English Benedictine Winifred (Bishop Boniface), to speed up the conversion of the Franks and the Germans.

The relationship with Charles Martel, mayor of the palace in the French kingdom, ended the Merovingian kingdoms in 722, which were replaced by the Carolingians. The Merovingians were murdered because the pope wanted to discontinue the line of the *Desposyni*.

After the death of Pope Paul I in 767, Duke Toto of Nepi appointed his own brother, who was not even a priest, as successor with the name Pope Constantine II. After consecration, he was opposed by many notables, who gouged out his eyes and locked him up in a monastery.

Desiderius, King of the Longobards, had been waiting for this and felt it was time for his own candidate to become pope. He appointed the monk Philip, who was ordained and installed on July 31, 768.

This pope was wise enough not to object (not wanting to have his eyes put out) and returned to his monastery cell.

The party that was inclined towards the Franks, headed by Pepin the Short, chose a Sicilian priest, who became Pope Stephen III. He denied the citizens of Rome the right to choose a pope themselves, claiming this right belonged to the clergy.

During the regime of his successor, Pope Hadrian I, King Charlemagne (Charles the Great) seized power in 774, by bringing to an end the two-hundred-year-old rule of the Longobards. He refused the pope any temporal authority or to cede territory to him. He had given himself the title "King of the Longobards" and in 781 he appointed his son Hadrian as King of Italy.

The next pope, Leo III, approached King Charlemagne with exaggerated humility, which greatly annoyed the noblemen. Their dislike was such, that his eyes were put out during a procession in 799, whereby he was nearly killed. Charlemagne took him under his wing and had him brought to Rome under safe guidance. He restored the order and the culprits were punished. The blind Pope Leo had found out that the Imperial throne in Byzantium was unoccupied. During Christmas midnight Mass, he suddenly placed a crown on the head of Charlemagne, knelt before him and requested the people to cheer for the new emperor.

But it turned out that Leo had been ill-informed. So, Charlemagne became only Emperor of the West. This shows that the papacy could not detach itself from the old thought of an imperial Church.

Under the pontificate of Sergius II (844-847), simony surfaced again. The trade in churchly titles and services brought in a lot of money. Sergius appointed, among others, his own brother, who was known to be corrupt, for the simple reason that he had sufficient wealth to pay the right price for his title.

When Leo IV was pope (847-855), there was a power struggle between the religious and temporal authorities.

The Church immediately brought forward the "Decretals" of the famous Church Father, Isidore of Seville. These documents can be compared to the "Donation of Constantine," except for the fact that this time, the forgers had been a lot smarter and practical. This fiat was supposed to demonstrate the supremacy of papal authority. The Decretals contained "evidence" that the spiritual power of the Pope of Rome was superior to worldly power and that this had been the case from the beginning of the primacy. Many popes demanded absolute power based on this decree, which was proven to be a forgery in the 14th century.

Pope John VIII was more of a soldier than a priest. He was revengeful and violent. In December 882, he himself was killed by members of his own family in an atrocious way because he had denied them the privileges to which they thought they had a right. When the cup of poison was not effective quickly enough, they crushed his skull with a hammer.

From this moment on, chaos reigned in Rome and in the Church. The historian Baronius called this the beginning of "the Night of the Papacy," a dark age that lasted until 1046. People fought to get churchly positions and the popes were scoundrels. The courtesans, voluptuous and cruel, used their charms to keep the gangs under control. No less than 48 popes in succession were puppets on the strings of a few rich families.

In May 896, Stephen VI became Pope. He was the son of a priest, and Pope Formosus (891- 896) had consecrated him as Bishop of Anagni. As a member of the Spoletians, he hated his predecessor for having the count of Spoleto removed from function. This psychopathic pope had the rotting corpse of Formosus dug up nine months after his death. He placed the corpse on a throne, vested it in papal robes and staged a macabre trial, the so-called "Cadaver Synod."

Formosus was posthumously accused of having been consecrated as Bishop of Rome while he was already Bishop of Porto – this was against the rules – and so this deranged man quashed Formosus' ordination as pope and thus invalidated all the ordinations he had performed upon others during his life.

The pope cut the fingers off the right hand of the corpse, the one that had been used to bless the crowds. Then he had the remains cast into a grave that held the corpses of foreigners. But this vengeful man was still not satisfied. He had the body dug up *again*, had the limbs removed and finally thrown into the Tiber.

The priests who were ordained by Formosus had finally had enough. They threw Stephen into a dungeon, where he was strangled in August 897.

In July 903, Leo V was ordained, but then imprisoned by September of that same year. This happened at the hands of Christopher, a priest who caused all sorts of intrigue and had Leo murdered. Christopher then took Leo's place, but Sergius killed him with his own hands in January 904, after a fake trial, and was ordained Sergius III on January 29th. He had been the main instigator of the "Cadaver Synod."

There were also some popes who were tricked by prostitutes, of whom they were lovers or sons.

In the beginning of the 10th century, the counts of Tusculum were able to impose their will on Rome. Godfather Theophylactus was a senator and the most prominent judge of the city. He was a powerful man, but his wife Theodora was even more powerful than he. They had two daughters, Theodora and Marozia, who very often frequented the Lateran Palace.

Marozia, fifteen years old, had set her heart on conquering the pope. Despite the fact that she was married to Alberic of Spoleto for two years, the 45-year-old pope was not averse to this young lady's charms. She bore him a son and made sure this son, Sergius, became pope later on.

This afore-mentioned adulterous "Holiness," Sergius III, was despicable, cruel and debauched. Thanks to the protection of Theodora and her two daughters he managed to maintain his position for seven years and died a rare, for that era, natural death.

Ten years before this, Theodora had taken notice of a public prosecutor for the Archbishop of Ravenna. Unable to resist, shortly after their first meeting he ended up in her bed – a great way to start a career in the Church! But Ravenna was too remote for the insatiable Theodora and that is why she made him Pope John X.

After her mother's death, Marozia took over her dominion. In May 928, she had the pope imprisoned and killed. Her current protégé and lover became Pope Leo VI, but after six months she had him bumped off too, to make way for her new lover, Stephen VII. He was then assassinated in February 931 and succeeded by her own son, Sergius (John XI).

Marozia had one ultimate dream: she wanted to become Queen or Empress. She was widowed now, and Hugo of Arles, the King of Italy, had also lost his wife. Because he was the brother of her second husband, however, a marriage between the two was legally impossible. Hugo devised a ruse and declared that both of his brothers were not of his bloodline. His brother Lambert did not accept this and therefore was murdered.

The new pope consecrated his mother's marriage, but the wedding turned out to be a dramatic event. Alberic junior, the son of her first husband, caused a scene and started to stir up the people against his new father-in-law. Hugo managed to escape and fled from Rome, but Marozia was chained and cast into a dungeon. The pope was not allowed to interfere. He was only permitted to offer quick prayers for his mother and was closely guarded. In this way, the female dominion in Rome that had lasted for thirty years came to an end.

However, the struggle for the primacy of the pope continued. On December 4, 963, Pope John XII was pushed aside by his successor Leo VIII. He was just a layman and was consecrated against all the rules.

John XII organized resistance and returned to Rome. Every enemy who fell into his hands had his eyes put out and his ears and nose cut off. Leo VIII managed to escape.

A wealthy Roman businessman came home earlier than expected one day and found a stranger in his bed, next to his wife. The lover retreated under the bed-covers, but was beaten repeatedly with a poker. When no more sounds came from beneath the covers, the husband pulled them away and threw the battered body out the window. This was how His Holiness Pope John XII died, on May 14th, 964.

In 972, Benedict VI became pope, against the will of Count Crescent, brother of the former Pope John XIII. He overpowered the pope and had him imprisoned. Then he quickly had Deacon Franco elected as the new pope.

In one of the his actions, Boniface VII, a man with a criminal temper, strangled his predecessor with his own hands. The Roman people revolted and he fled to Constantinople, taking with him the treasures of Saint Peter's Basilica. Thirteen years later, when the emperor died, Boniface VII returned to Rome. With the support of Crescent junior, the current pope was killed, and he placed himself on the papal throne once more; but a year later, in that seemingly endless cycle, it was his turn.

Boniface VII was succeeded by John XV, who incurred the clergy's hatred for his greed and nepotism. John XV was the pope who introduced canonization by elevating Ulric of Augsburg in 993.

Pope Benedict VIII had the "Creed" (from *Credo*: "I believe") definitively incorporated as part of the liturgy in Holy Mass.

His brother Alberic, a doorman, succeeded him as Pope John XIX. He was ordained as a priest and then pope in just one day.

In 1032, Benedict IX became pope when he was a little over twelve years old, but certainly less than fifteen. His family had paid the obligatory sum so he could succeed his uncles. He was a thief and a murderer, following the example of his ancestors Theodora and Marozia.

From the Papal Annals it appears that he ascended the throne three times: in December 1032, February 1045, and November 1047. The citizens of Rome had already enough of him in 1036 and wanted to take his life, which was one of horror and scandal. When the Archbishop of Milan denounced the papal morals, he was banished by Benedict IX. In 1044 the people revolted. The Pope was chased away and the tiara was sold to the highest bidder.

Sylvester III became pope in January 1045, but in February Benedict returned and was officially re-elected in April. A problem arose when he wanted to marry the daughter of Gerard of Galeria, the captain of the insurgents who had expelled him. An ingenious and irreproachable priest, John Graziano, gave him the valuable advice to sell his Papal Office. By way of an official deed of sale, he sold his office for 1500 silver pounds, with the guarantee of a large annual allowance as well as the hand of Gerald's daughter.

John Graziano then became Pope Gregory VI. The abbot of Cluny and the holy hermit, Gunther of Niedertach, called on King Henri II of France to take responsibility and consecrate a pope who would bring honor to the office. A synod was held, where the fate of the squabbling popes was sealed: Benedict IX was expelled, Sylvester III was sent back to his diocese, and Gregory VI was banished to Cologne.

For centuries, the relations between the Pope of Rome and the Patriarch of Constantinople had been disturbed by theological differences of opinion that were hard to reconcile. Besides that, there were differences in language, tradition and cultural sensitivities. The new patriarch, Michael Cerularius, accused the Western Christians of heresy and wanted to have the Latin churches and monasteries shut down.

Pope Leo IX strongly protested and sent a delegation to Constantinople. They received a very cold welcome there, with the result that the patriarch was excommunicated by the pope. The patriarch, in turn, then banished the pope. This caused a definitive break between the Western and Eastern Churches.

The cardinalate was instituted, and the omnipotent Cardinal Hildebrand made sure that henceforth, the pope would be elected by and from the group of cardinals. The people, the lower clergy and the emperor himself were relegated to the role of giving their consent after the fact. The papal power had grown stronger.

Pope Alexander II died on April 21, 1073, and Hildebrand hesitated not a moment to grab power and had himself "elected" by the people. He was ordained on the same day as the cardinals' Pope Gregory VII. His collaborators called this pope "the Holy Satan." He turned the papacy into a world dictatorship. He did not try to hide his feelings of vengeance towards the emperor's son, because the last one had taken such a strong stance against simony under Gregory VI. This pope himself did not recoil from anything, not even letting the city of Rome burn to the ground. In a fanatic way, he wanted to give the power and glory back to the papacy that was dishonored and placed under guardianship.

This presumptuous potentate recorded a number of rules in his *Dictatus Papae*.

Some examples:

1. Only the Roman Church was created by God.

2. Only the Bishop of Rome can call himself ecumenical.

3. Only he can consecrate or depose Bishops or grant mercy.

9. All Princes must kiss the Pope's feet.

12. The Pope has the right to dethrone Emperors.

18. Nobody can invalidate his decisions; he alone can nullify sentences.

19. Nobody can judge him.

22. The Roman Church has never made mistakes and, according to the testimony of the Bible, also cannot make mistakes.

It became his obsession to free the papacy from any competing authority and place the pope at the summit of the pyramid.

In 1074, he organized a council meeting and ordered every priest who had been ordained due to simony, to leave the Church. Every bishop who had bought his office had to resign or else be excommunicated. The people were obliged to no longer attend any mass that was celebrated by a married priest.

In 1075, the pope again called a council together, in which five bishops from the immediate environs of Holy Roman Emperor King Henri IV were deposed. This was the onset of the "Battle of Investiture," which would last for about 50 years.

Many cardinals were annoyed by Gregory's autocratic behavior. He only accepted advice from three women: Empress Agnes, Beatrice of Tuscany, and her daughter, Countess Mathildis. The Battle of Investiture was fought publicly between pope and king. The king called together a council of bishops and Gregory was relieved from office. The Archbishop of Ravenna became the Anti-pope Clemens III. The king besieged the city of Rome, but Gregory refused to leave. However, in June 1083, Godfrey of Bouillon took the Papal Guard by surprise, after which Gregorius fled.

Clemens III was consecrated as Pope and in his turn crowned the king as Emperor. It would take 130 years for peace to come, because the Church was often saddled with two popes and squeezed between the armies of the emperor and those of the Vikings.

In 1154, the first and only English pope was ordained as Hadrian IV. He was the son of a priest, who had fled to the monastery in order to escape his temporal fatherly duties. As a result, he had to go begging early in his life in order to survive. He embarked for France and did manual labor for the monks of Saint Raf. There he became a monk, then a prior and finally abbot. He wanted to reorganize the abbey and wrote a letter to the pope, who summoned him and ordained him as a cardinal.

Pope Hadrian wrote to the king in England that he had to be aware of the fact that Ireland and the other islands were under the authority of Rome. He wanted worldly power, and the king as well as the Norsemen would experience this.

The clergy eliminated any form of municipal freedom and the people hated them for it. The Pope was no longer allowed to enter the Lateran Palace and had to settle with normal lodgment. When a cardinal was stabbed in the middle of a busy street, the Pope intervened. He enunciated the "Interdict" which was the first time a pope made use of this extreme means. Mass was no longer celebrated, bells were no longer tolled, there was no baptism, not even blessing, and there were no wedding ceremonies. At first, the Romans remained undisturbed, but no Holy Mass was celebrated at Easter. Four days after Easter, the senators went down on their knees and begged the pope to lift this unbearable sanction. Hadrian agreed, under the condition that they would hand over to him the leader of the progressionists who had led the revolt of the people. The people sacrificed their leader and the pope came back to his Lateran Palace.

At the end of the 12th century, people were already becoming more aware and started to fight for freedom: democracy versus monarchy, Church versus empire, popular religion versus papacy. Italy became the birthplace of municipal freedom, republics were born, and Rome blossomed, economically as well as artistically. Outside the city, the pope could design the world according to his wishes, but inside Rome his power was no longer tolerated.

The 13th century distinguished itself by the reign of Pope Innocent III, who came to power in 1198. He became the most powerful pope in history, claiming absolute hegemony. He brought grandeur to the papacy, but at the end of this same century Boniface VIII caused the downfall of it all.

For his coronation, Innocent III organized a prestigious procession, with pomp and circumstance which marched from Saint Peter's to the Lateran Palace. The procession consisted of churchly sovereigns, lawyers, and judges. They were all on horseback, but only the pope rode a white horse. The procession was cheered by the people, while all of the church bells in Rome produced a deafening thunder.

On November 11, 1215, the Fourth Lateran Council began. It was the crowning glory of Innocent's work. 1,500 Prelates attended and knelt in front of him. He had reached his goal: Absolute Power in the Church.

Innocent was a man who coldly despised his subjects. He had an unquenchable thirst for power and made use of a certain form of terrorism to enforce his authority.

After Innocent III politics predominated, and actual religion moved more into the background. This brought nothing but disillusionment. All leaders were divided among themselves and the fifth crusade, instigated by the successor, Pope Honorius III, was a failure. There was now resistance among the Christians themselves, because they generally disapproved of the crusade against their fellow Christians, the Albigensians, that had been conducted with so much cruelty.

The massacres that followed during the Inquisition also did not add to the popes' prestige, but they kept on in their morbid fanaticism.

On June 25, 1243, Innocent IV was chosen. He had absolutist ideas, was stubborn and unscrupulous. In 1244, the pope was warned of a fleet of ships nearing the coast, with 300 knights on board. They were coming to depose and imprison him. He dressed himself as a soldier, fled to Lyon and sought protection from the French king.

He called for a council, in which the emperor was held accountable for all the ills the Christians had to endure.

Frederic II was dethroned, and his Kingdom of Sicily was taken over. Frederic pointed out the great danger of the popes to the world with these words: "I am neither the first nor the last that was dethroned by priestly abuse of power. If you obey these hypocrites, to whom all the water in the Jordan would not be enough to quench their thirst for power, you are an accomplice to their wrongdoings."

This papal brute, Innocent IV, supported Cardinal Rainer's plan to kill Frederic II and his son Enzio.

During this latest horrible regime, the pope's prestige was severely damaged. Innocent IV was hypocritical and greedy. He gave the inquisitors permission to torture and took the right to appeal away from the convicts.

His last words were as unworthy as his life. On his deathbed he said to his family: "Why are you sitting there, complaining? Have I not made you rich enough?"

In 1277, Nicholas III was elected as the new pope. He was the son of a violent senator and distinguished himself by always letting his personal interests prevail. He was a real Roman, who measured "greatness" by the amount of acquired treasure. His family was immensely privileged, for his nepotism was without boundaries. Dante included this pope in Hell for his simony and nepotism.

In the beginning of 1292, Rome experienced complete anarchy. There was pillaging, church possessions were stolen, and pilgrims were murdered. It was time to elect a new pope, but the cardinals could not come to an agreement. On August 24, 1294, Celestine V, totally unqualified for the task, was crowned as the new pope. He was a hermit, who had lived in complete seclusion for thirty years. Without any choice, he was forced to become pope – otherwise he would not have survived. Pope Celestine was weak, mentally unstable and not able to handle the power-hungry hordes of the Vatican.

His advisor Cardinal Benedetto Caetani created a new precedent by, for the first time in Church history, forcing the pope to abdicate his throne. Out of gratitude, Caetani was consecrated as Pope Boniface VIII in December.

Unfortunately, the incompetent was replaced by yet another Pontiff with an insatiable hunger for power and personal wealth. He made many enemies and, in 1297, was warned to withdraw himself. He reacted by banishing two cardinals, demolishing their birthplaces completely and confiscating all their goods.

In 1309 Pope Clemens V, a Frenchman, moved operations from Rome to Avignon, where the papal authority would stay for seventy years. There they continued to engage in nepotism and lived in unprecedented wealth.

During the papacy of Clemens V, blatant corruption reigned side-by-side with the trade in churchly offices and simony.

Pope Clemens VI was a squanderer and brought the Church to financial ruin.

His successor, Innocent VI, tried to end the corruption and abuses. He asked the Roman Curia to live more soberly and limit its expenses. Apparently, though, nepotism missed the list on his reform agenda; he did not hesitate to favor his own family with rich rewards. His successor, Urban V, got permission to return to Rome, but when he arrived there in 1367 the city was in ruins and had been burned to the ground. His Vatican palace was so austere that, after three years of relatively Spartan conditions, he returned to the luxury of Avignon. A female beggar predicted that he would soon die if he left Rome and, indeed, he did a few months later.

In 1378, the Neapolitan, Prignano, was elected as Pope Urban VI. Another arrogant despot, he treated his cardinals in an aggressive and presumptuous way. He scolded them and had no intention of letting them return to Avignon. The French cardinals hated him and finally fled. In co-operation with the current Anti-pope Gregory XI, who held residence in a fortified castle in Anagni, they drew up a manifesto that annulled the election of Urban VI. They elected Clemens VII, and he took his residence in Avignon.

During the 52 years that followed there was a great schism. The battling popes in Rome and Avignon kept banishing one another, like children on a playground. "Am too!" Are Not!" Etc., etc. None of them was reliable and in the end, all of Western Christianity was excommunicated. Confusion reigned supreme over all reason.

Urban VI was an extremely wasteful man, who mismanaged his affairs. He became unacceptable for his social environment, started drinking to extreme excess and went completely insane. He had cardinals tortured. Some were put in a bag that was sewn up and thrown into the sea, and others were buried alive.

His successor Boniface IX made good use of Urban's proclamation that 1390 was a Holy Year. He motivated people with the terrors of everlasting Hell in order to make them come to Rome for the Jubilee, where they could avoid damnation by buying an indulgence at the highest possible price. This old reliable smoke-and-mirrors routine worked like a charm and the proceeds of the Jubilee enabled him to turn the Vatican into a stronghold of power. This is the origin of the expression: "Sometimes one has to pay a high price for something."

Neither the cardinals in Avignon nor Rome had the will to end the schism. They kept electing new competing popes, who would promise to end it, but once on the papal throne and confronted with political reality, they forgot to do so very quickly.

In 1409, during the Council of Pisa, both Pope Benedict XIII and Gregory XII were accused of schismatic behavior, perjury, heresy, and ordered to abdicate office, which they ignored. The council then elected the Anti-pope Alexander V and, *hey presto*, there were suddenly three popes! Alexander died only a few months later – probably by poisoning – and then there were two.

On May 17, 1410, Balthasar Cossa was elected as Anti-pope John XXIII. He was known as a dangerous man, because he was an infamous murderer, who had already poisoned two popes. Although Balthasar was of noble descent, he led a lawless life enriching himself as a pirate in the Mediterranean. He became archbishop thanks to his influential family and discovered that the trade in indulgences and usury yielded even more loot than piracy, without the risks. He therefore bought his cardinalship and thus ascended to the papacy.

He called a council in order to strengthen his position, but the result was disastrous. In 1414, the Council of Constance decided that Popes Gregory XII and Benedict XIII should abdicate. John XXIII was himself accused of simony and convicted for the scandalous life he had led prior to his election.

John tried to flee, but he was imprisoned and deprived of his rights. It took months until Gregory was prepared to doff the tiara. Only Benedict kept resisting, because he wanted to die as a pope. He promised to withdraw to his fortified castle on the Peniscola peninsula. Until his death in 1423, he was the conductor of something resembling an operetta-version of the papacy.

On November 11, 1417, the great Western Schism was finally over, when Martin V was elected as sole pope. Immediately, a new conflict was born – the battle between the council and a pope who no longer accepted that the council surpassed him. But the council had become aware of its power and wasn't keen to give it up.

Martin V rebuilt Rome and thereby earned this epitaph: *The happiness of his century*. The shadow-side to his papacy was that ubiquitous sin, nepotism. He kept up the tradition by favoring his family members with the rich rewards of theocratic office.

The struggle between the council and the pope continued during the pontificate of his successor, Eugenius IV, and it was not until 1449 at the Council of Basel that Pope Nicholas V achieved victory; the Papacy was freed from all forms of examination and, in the following years, it appeared impossible to re-introduce a democratic process. The characters of the men seated on the papal throne continued to fall short of spiritual purity. They abused their power when and wherever they pleased, and led bizarre lives.

It was not until a century later that the Council of Trent (1545-1563) set straight what had gone wrong in Basel in 1449.

Between these two councils reigned popes who, by abuse of their power, caused irreparable tragedies. They were responsible for the first opening of the Great Schism that splintered Western Christianity. An era dawned of great inner and outer discord and disorder – an era in which nepotism became an institution. The popes lived in extreme luxury; their moral authority was a transparent mockery, and the worship of Mammon became their only true religion. To pay for this ever-mounting avarice, the trade in indulgences was intensified, while they were busy indulging *themselves* with women, orgies, intrigue, crime, sadism and dirty politics.

The papal tiara was pawned regularly at the banks in Rome, whenever the treasury of the Vatican reached rock-bottom.

Preceding the papal election, shameless vote-trading took place in titles, palaces, and incomes. The wealthy and noble courtesans used sex and influence to play the cardinals off against each other. They knew how to flatter them, seduce them and extract their secrets, which, in exchange for large sums of money, they swapped with other cardinals in between the sheets. There was blackmail, thievery and murder. The age-old stew of iniquity.

Rome was in total anarchy. To fill his treasury, Pope Innocent VIII allowed criminals to avoid the death penalty by paying a fine.

This pope was also guilty of one of the great atrocities in history. He gave vent to his sadistic hatred of women by accusing them of having sex with the devil – they were *witches*. As a result, they underwent violent torture and were sometimes burned alive. There are not enough words to describe how the clergy treated women in those days. They were used and then murdered.

Pope "Innocent" had the philosopher Pico della Mirandola killed because he planned to make a statement about the dignity of the individual.

After the death of Innocent VIII in July 1492, the Holy See of Saint Peter was auctioned in order to raise money. Rodrigo Borgia was the highest bidder. With his huge wealth, he managed to bribe five of the twenty-three other cardinals, which put him over the top. As Pope Alexander VI, he literally opened the Gates of Hell. He had three children by an unknown mother. He attracted women like a magnet, until Vannozza dei Cattanei managed to tie him down. He married her off to three subsequent husbands, who covered up for him and were rewarded with a position in the Roman Curia. When Alexander VI became pope, Vannozza declared he was the father of her four surviving children.

Alexander hosted heathen Bacchic festivities (orgies) in the great Cathedral itself.

Giovanni de Medici received his first ordinations shortly before he was consecrated as pope. Under the name of Leo X, he was crowned on April 11, 1513. During this celebration, Rome was transformed to a grand exposition of heathen gods. This pope adored Mars, Venus and Pallas Athena. He loved the theatrical aspect of it all.

He felt he should not be diverted by petty religious matters. "God wanted us to become Pope, so why not enjoy the Papacy?" was his motto.

His position as head of the Medici family seemed more important to him than his function as sovereign of the Church. Under his reign, aggressive nepotism reached new heights. He deposed dukes and offered their thrones to his family members. He had huge palaces built for his family and, to finance these, he ordered in 1514 the sale of indulgences for souls in purgatory, all over Europe. A Dominican named Tetzel was the star promoter of this trade. The maxim that resounded everywhere was: "When the florin reaches the bottom of the money box, the soul jumps straight from purgatory to heaven."

For the Augustinian monk Luther this was all to excessive. In 1517, he literally and physically nailed down his immediately notorious 95 *Theses* against the great swindle in indulgences, and other spiritual abuse. He was soon in a theological fist-fight with Roman Catholic headquarters.

The sparring went on until, on December 10, 1520, Luther publicly burned the letter of excommunication he had received, and the wars of the Reformation were kindled. During the term of Pope Clemens VII (1523-1534), the schism soon resulted in Henry VIII's declaration of independence for the English Church (albeit mainly for personal reasons).

Clemens' successor Paul III was a lawless cardinal before becoming pope and he had fathered many children with several women. During his papacy, the pope and his cardinals enjoyed themselves with licentious parties, masquerades and other questionable spectacles.

Pope Julius III, who came after him, continued this tradition. This pope's favorite pastime was to preside over all kinds of heathen festivities.

Like a rude splash of cold water, Pope Pius V's reign was different from that of his predecessors. He was ascetically inclined and lived a strict and sober life. He made sure the priests were actually trained in seminaries and during his papacy the first known *Catechism* was published in 1566.

The scales were tipped to the other extreme. Rome became like a monastery, or even a reformatory.

Pius took a fanatical stance toward any person who refused to accept Rome's dogma. His battle against heretics was ruthless. His expression was: "No pity! No more reconciliations! Exterminate those who subject themselves as well as those who resist. Persecute them to the utmost, kill and burn them, set everything on fire and avenge the Lord." In his theological holocaust prostitutes and adulterous women were also arrested and killed.

In 1592, Clemens VIII became the pope. The sisters Beatrice and Lucrezia, both in their early twenties, were decapitated in Rome during his reign. What was the case?

Their father had held his family captive for years in a fortress in Rieti. He tortured his wife and abused his daughters. One day, the girls managed to kill their father and so put an end to the hell in which they lived, but the pope remained inflexible: the girls had murdered their father and therefore they deserved capital punishment. The people lynched the officially blameless executioner, because they could not vent their anger on the pope.

Like a vicious circle, there was no end to the morbid behavior of the popes and the other Church fathers. It went on and on.

During the pontificate of Innocent X, there was a female crypto-pope: Olimpia Maidalchini. Overbearing and loud in nature, with an insatiable thirst for wealth, she was the widow of the pope's brother and firmly took charge. Innocent had no authority and feared her. Olimpia instituted a provocative law in 1645: "During important ceremonies, whores were granted permission to be carried in a state-carriage. Because of the gifts she received from them, Donna Olimpia had decided to take them under her care and she even allowed them to adorn their carriage with her own insignia…." There was, as usual, much ostentation and scandalous intrigue. The lust for power, money and loose behavior seems to have been injected as a virus into the DNA of Europe's ruling class, and there was never an end to it.

With the death of Innocent X, the power of this female pope also came to an end.

From 1790, the Roman Church gradually lost more of its former monopoly on power. The bishops in Germany distanced themselves from the papal dominion. In revolutionary France, the state seized all churchly goods, took away the clergy's established rights and dissolved all monastic orders. In 1792, 300 priests were executed and about 40,000 clergymen fled abroad.

In February 1798, the French general Berthier conquered the city of Rome. He took away all worldly power from Pope Pius VI and proclaimed the Italian Republic. The pope was imprisoned, banished from Italy, and died in 1799. Napoleon needed 500 carriages to transport the treasures he seized to Paris.

All cardinals fled to Venice, where they elected a new pope: Pius VII. Because the majority of the French people were Catholic, Napoleon needed the cooperation of the clergy and the pope to restore unity. He claimed the right to manage all churchly possessions. He sent soldiers to Rome and took five provinces out of the Papal State, which he then added to Italy.

Napoleon made clear in a letter to Pius VII that he should be grateful to have no more worldly power. Therefore, he could dedicate himself much better to his true calling, the pastoral service. Pius replied by excommunicating all "villains" who had robbed the "inheritance of Peter." This pope was also captured and taken to France. After Napoleon's return from his ill-advised Russian campaign, his empire crumbled and Pius returned to Rome in 1814.

Leo XII, who succeeded him, turned the clock back to the Middle Ages. He immediately eliminated the progressive Cardinal Consalvi, who advocated tolerance and freedom. The Inquisition and the witch-hunt were revived and proponents of a unified Italy were eliminated. He fanatically punished everybody who resisted him.

The Jews were once more placed in ghettos and their possessions were confiscated. They were forced to listen to endless sermons, ostensibly to open their minds to the Roman Catholic truth, but really more a form of brainwashing, which had no effect except to instill fear of punishment. He prohibited inoculation against smallpox, because he felt this to be an invention of the devil.

His successors Gregory XVI and Pius IX were no different. In March 1861, Victor-Emmanuel became King of Italy. He proposed a reformation of the Papal State, but Pius IX was not having any.

In 1870, the Churchly State disappeared, because Rome was overrun by the Piedmontese. The pope continuously excommunicated all sorts of people, but to no avail. He proclaimed himself to be a prisoner of the Vatican. The Catholics saw him as a martyr and conservative movements appeared in several countries which offered him support.

The papal encyclical "*Quanta Curia*" of 1856, condemned all modern ideas. A yawning gap appeared between contemporaries and the Church became divided. This defeat was hard to accept, and their failing grasp on worldly power incited the Church to proclaim papal infallibility during the Vatican Council in 1869, in an attempt to gain back some status. It was an arrogant proclamation which bore witness to the fact that the pope did not like to lose face.

At the council, 57 members planned to vote against the proclamation, but the vote was cancelled when the Franco-Prussian War broke out and many had to return to France and Germany. The greater part of the remaining opponents were Italians – they were poor and financially dependent upon the pope. The pope informed them that if they voted against infallibility, they would no longer receive basic necessities. Only two members present voted against the proclamation, and so this ridiculous dogma became official Church policy.

Three years after Pius IX died, at night and under police protection, his remains were transferred to Saint-Laurens-outside-the-Walls. However, this did not prevent people who had sworn to "Cast this bastard into the Tiber!" from shouting insults at the funeral procession.

His successor Leo XIII had studied philosophy, theology and law. He wanted the clergy to focus more on Christian philosophy and the Bible. In 1881, he opened the Vatican Archives to the public.

His successor Pius X, however, was an opponent of modern ideas. In 1910, every candidate for priesthood was obliged to take the "anti-modernism oath." In addition, all Catholics were banned from reading magazines that were "non-approved" by the Church.

Pope Pius XI was elected in 1922, the same year Mussolini's "Black Shirts" undertook the march to Rome. A concordat was reached on February 11, 1929, in which the papacy acknowledged the Kingdom of Italy, with Rome as its capital. For renouncing its former State, the Church received 1,750,000,000 lire and an enclave of about 110 acres (Vatican City). As a result, the Church could officially engage in diplomatic relations with other states.

The concordat between the Vatican and Germany, which was signed on July 20, 1931, had a conveniently ambiguous meaning for Adolph Hitler, who became Chancellor in March 1933. Both he and Mussolini had an interest in being recognized by the highest moral authority.

The pope protested Nazi policies 34 times, but Hitler ignored him. He even ignored the encyclical "Mit Brennender Sorge" (with burning concern). His real answer was a secret persecution of Catholics.

At the command of Mussolini, Pius XI was assassinated in February 1939.

His successor, Pius XII, became known as ascetic and "silent." His silence with regard to the atrocities of the Second World War was certainly remarkable. With the knowledge of this craven puppet-pope, hundreds of thousands fell victim to a quick or slow death, for their nationality, politics, religion, or race.

After the war, the Vatican even helped fascist war criminals escape to South America.

The next pope, John XXIII, was a reformer who gave the Church a more humane image and tried to redistribute some of the Church's vast wealth. His charisma stemmed from the fact that he remained a true and humble human-being at all times. He died on June 3, 1963, of stomach cancer.

His successor, Paul VI, was no advocate of the changes his predecessor had made. As the pendulum swung once more to the right, he discontinued this approach and his pontificate did not have much impact except as a placeholder.

In 1978, 65-year-old Venetian patriarch Albino Luciani was elected as Pope John Paul I. He was the kind of man one could compare to Gandhi or Martin Luther King. Contrary to many previous popes, who exercised their power over a significant part of the world population, John Paul I with his loving appearance, was not directly the epitome of such power.

Most people thought he was an intermediate pope of little importance, but insiders knew this Luciani was getting ready to introduce revolutionary changes. During the 33 days of his brief pontificate, he instigated reforms across the board which would have had great benefit to all of humanity.

Alas, his life did not last long. Vultures and power-crazed elitists like Bishop (and Vatican Bank director) Paul Marcinkus, and Cardinal Jean Villot, did not want their monopoly broken by this upstart pope, whom they perversely saw as a bigot. So, this honest man had to be removed. They carried out a plot, devised by the Vatican medical service and Cardinal Villot.

John Paul I died under very suspicious circumstances, and to this day no death certificate has been made public, despite repeated requests. After a cursory visual examination it took the Vatican physician only a few minutes to announce the cause of death as a heart attack. No other doctor could be found willing to take responsibility for this diagnosis; no autopsy was performed, and all subsequent requests were refused. Cardinal Villot had his reasons. Afterwards, the cause of death was completely contradicted by other experts.

The American journalist David Yallop undertook an extensive examination and presented his conclusions in his book, *In God's Name*. The financial connections between the Church and the Mafia are also thoroughly discussed.

The history of papacy is a disastrous one, because many criminals and fanatics left their marks on it. Alas, there were very few exceptions of popes who were straight.

As a reasonable human being, knowing this history, I can hardly imagine anyone as a priest, bishop, cardinal or pope functioning honestly within this repeatedly criminal and chronically deceitful organization.

GNOSTICISM

Of all texts I came across during my search for the truth, the books describing the old knowledge, Gnosticism, intrigued me most. The researcher and scientist, Professor Gilles Quispel, comes to mind, as well as author Jacob Slavenburg. While I was reading their books, one surprise followed another. It was all so logical that I immediately felt, "Yes, this is how it works." The pieces of the puzzle kept falling into place. Gradually, I discovered the elements which the early Catholic Church used to implement their distortions of the historical truth.

I also discovered that the historical figure of Jesus was the greatest Gnostic of all times. He was a seer, a human being of high sensitivity, a light-worker, who carried all knowledge and wisdom within himself. He wanted to make the people conscious and learn that we are connected to the Father, the all-embracing Light, the All. We are all part of the All, because our spirit is part of this Light.

The word gnosis means knowledge from within, knowledge from the heart and teaches us that all is one, that the Divine is present in everything and in every person. Everybody is, so to speak, like a spark of the great whole. The best philosophical minds we know were in fact Gnostics, because they were aware of this.

For Gnostics, the idea of being born again in a different body was normal. They taught us that the spirit (pneuma) is everlasting. Our physical existence is a process we have to go through in order to improve and perfect ourselves.

The Church was of no concern to the Gnostic, because he did not need a priest or a saint to act as intermediary between man and the Divine. He forms the All-embracing in himself! Gnosis is a universal knowledge and is not connected to any form of organized religion. It is something that has always been and always will be, because it is a part of human nature. Religion, however, has been artificially created by us, and it replaces the inner experience with the external form. The religious movement called Catholicism has regarded Gnosticism as hostile from the start, because it confronted them with their own falsehoods. Religion is impure, because it is connected to the human ego.

The concepts of *light* and *dark* are central to the Gnostic teachings. These are the two elementary and essential principles of our human development.

The *light* is connected to our subconscious. Once we are aware of this, we start to understand what life is about. It usually takes a long time to let go of the duality within ourselves. After this we reach the stage of complete balance, also referred to as *enlightenment*.

Darkness refers to everything that has to do with the material side of existence. Character traits play an important role in this, things like inflexibility and greed.

Light and darkness are opposites, but at the same time they can go hand in hand – if they are connected by balance. Gnosticism is quite clear about that. If you wish to reach this stage, it is important to open up to your feelings. This means that you have to open up to your *higher self*. From this, automatically flows the recognition that there is a source of Life, which is also a source of guidance.

Jesus of Sirach, an important philosopher, was the author of a Gnostic writing which was omitted from the Bible. I quote: "He gave them knowledge and they inherited the law of life." *He* refers to the All. When we have been given knowledge (gnosis) and we have gained insight, we come to realize that we have to act from this richness deep within ourselves. These inspiring words of Jesus of Sirach have the power to awaken echoes in our deepest being.

We can use the insight we have gained in order to penetrate deeper into our hearts. That is where one finds the Source and we can experience and love it. We start to realize that nothing in the world is more important. As a result, you peel off the ego still further and then let go of it, in order to get closer to the Source. In this way, we become aware of the fact that we are, ourselves, part of the Light and that is our heritage! This is how we receive the law of life. We get to know the meaning of all, which the Source expresses in a loving creation. It is an everlasting treaty which has been made with each living being. *To create* means to form a bond with that which is created.

The Gospel of Thomas is, without question, a Gnostic writing. In it we find many statements Jesus made.

For example: "If a blind and a sighted person are together in the darkness, then they do not differ from each other. But when the light comes, the sighted person will see it, and the blind one will remain in darkness."

All of us are probably familiar with the expression, *having seen the light*, but we speak these words without realizing them. It actually does not refer to having seen the light with our physical eyes. It means, to gain insight. It is like shutters have been opened and suddenly we can see the real essence of some life aspects. Consider *A Christmas Carol*, Dickens' much-beloved story of Ebenezer Scrooge. After a life of misery and avarice, on Christmas Eve he takes a harrowing dream-journey through the denials and mistakes of his past, his present isolated unhappiness, and the dire consequences coming in the future. His eyes open to the truth, and on Christmas morning he wakes to a new and joyous consciousness. The light *within* him has been relit and good will has prevailed.

In the same text of the Gospel of Thomas, Jesus says: "A person with light in the soul enlightens the world. Without light in the soul, there is darkness."

The *light* that is being referred to here, is the basic principle of our existence. When you become conscious of this inner beacon, it will change the direction of your life. For the Gnostic, darkness equals the world of limited thinking, without enlightenment. It is a world filled with illusions, uncertainties, false promises, tiredness and compulsive behavior. It is characterized by pain and misery. In short, this is the world we are all familiar with. The Gnostic knows very well that this world is not his original home. We could say that the Gnostic wakes up by his insight, while others remain asleep. Because when we keep placing our trust in our intellect and see our surroundings as the only real existence, our lives will stay limited to the material aspect.

Some time ago, the late Pieter de Boer (professor emeritus of philosophy in Leiden) remarked during an interview: "Wisdom and imagination are more important than knowledge and information." An interesting statement, because it is true that the inner knowing is far more important. I think everyone, at a certain point in time, must let go of denial of the inner experience and duality, which arises from being. Because only then, can the inner light to which the Gnostic refers can be ignited.

By being aware of this, we own it and start to emit it. The Light in us becomes stronger and we get closer to the Light of Life. We then will reach our inner core. This awakens the Christ consciousness.

The Gospel of Thomas says: "Whoever has come to know the world, has discovered a carcass, and whoever has discovered this carcass, has risen beyond this world."

This is clear language, because he who knows the world, is able to rise above the material aspect of things.

The fact that every human being is part of the Life Principle is anchored in gnosis. From the point of view that this insight is the foundation of reality, light is shed over a large spectrum, which would remain closed if we kept seeing the material as the only purpose. In the eyes of the Gnostic, a birth is the incarnation of a soul that starts a new path of development. When we keep considering the outside world as reality, we will always be confronted with disappointment, pain and sorrow.

We live in a world filled with structures and material truths, invented by people and blown up like castles in the air. It is great to have a good life and to enjoy it; there is nothing wrong with that, but the essence is about the way you deal with it! We can get attached to our material possessions, but we can also view them as no more than utensils.

By reading Gnostic writings, we come to the conclusion that detachment liberates us and brings us more inner peace.

Jesus says, in the Gospel of Thomas: "I am the way!" What he means is that he is an example. "I am the life!" means he is at one with the life-giving Light.

Sometimes, one wonders how it is possible that certain Christian factions have the nerve to use words like the "ones who are lost." It is not only arrogant and shameful, but also humiliating. So, if a person does not belong to their religious faction, he is lost! But there are no such things as heaven, hell and purgatory. Nobody gets lost, because every soul is part of the Light and will eventually return there. The Western world is governed by the fear of death. After all, we do not know what will happen to us after we die, and since the Holy Church has employed indoctrination and threats on us for centuries, we never know if we have lived our life in a (sufficiently) good manner! This fear is so strong, that people even have trouble surrendering to death. Everybody knows our physical existence is finite, but at the same time people do not like to ponder this subject.

Our existence is founded on great wisdom, which has been completely suppressed by our rational thinking. It is good to realize that we depend on a Source that controls our lives. Everybody can experience this, but it can be hard to accept when we think about it. Many people have trouble dealing with this and avoid it, even when they regularly experience that certain things develop along different and unexpected pathways from what they thought they wanted. This creates a struggle, because unfortunately not everybody can accept life the way it happens. The knowledge inside us and our inner experience of this, leads to growing awareness. The Gnostic views his inner knowledge as a personal good, which he has earned by learning processes in previous lives. This inner knowledge lives on, recorded in the deeper layers of his consciousness. By allowing self-knowledge to play a part in daily life, the Gnostic acknowledges the Christ within himself. The result is an attitude to life that is more positive and balanced.

The Christians only speak of the Christ outside themselves, as a title for Jesus, while the Gnostics experience the Christ within themselves. According to ecclesiastical dogma, Jesus is the savior; but salvation has to be found within ourselves – we can save ourselves.

This knowledge was dangerous to the Roman Catholic Church. By being untouchable and furthermore by weaving a spell of mystery which defied understanding by the average citizen, the Church turned its ideas into myths. This was easier, because the ideas were well protected and not negotiable. People kept hearing sayings like "you have to believe this, because it is the Word of God," and this was the reason the human soul kept moving away from its eventual goal: enlightenment.

But the Church had misjudged! Gnosticism was kept alive during all the centuries. Even theological and philosophical science could not ignore it. This was most obvious during the Renaissance. The term *gnosis* was avoided, because it was not accepted within Catholic Christian thinking in those days. It was therefore called Neo-Platonism, because Plato taught us that outside the sensory-perceptible cosmos, there is a world that is eternal and imperishable that could only be observed from a contemplative perspective. To Plato, everything was a gift from higher realms and he was very aware of the fact that we are connected to everything around us. Aside from that, people were, during this period, very interested in the thought of revelation – a philosophical body of ideas based on the idea of reincarnation.

By using the Church as a means to find deliverance, we automatically identify ourselves with the specific interests of this organization and support its right to exist. This institution of the Church has always been the cause of ideological conflict, resulting in groups of people fighting each other. Fortunately, we are now in the privileged position of having freedom of religion and freedom of opinion. Therefore, we can rightfully question things like *writings inspired by God, the Word of God, Papal Infallibility and dogma.*

Since the 1960's, people's interest in attending religious services has gradually dwindled. Many people have distanced themselves from the Christian churches, because they did not cope with the changing times.

Moreover, something that is based upon lies is doomed to eventually disappear. These Churches suffer from tunnel vision and their dogma is oppressive.

Gnosticism still exists, but since we are not familiar with it, we do not recognize the term. We use different terms for it. Gnosticism is the same as what we now know as spirituality or consciousness.

It is a deep, spiritual experience when we realize we are particles of the Light, which is the core of Gnosticism. Of course, it does not mean we start to float around. On the contrary, we start to experience reality in a deeper way and gain more respect for the life that surrounds us.

In the last half-century, people's interest in spirituality has grown enormously. We can conclude this from the many books published in this field and from the rise of esoteric centers and shops. People are not only looking for answers, they also feel the need for profundity and conduct their own search for the essence of existence. Apart from that, people remain curious and want to find out what the future might bring. Current spirituality leads us back to personal experience. It allows people the space to find the Light by way of a personal quest, because this is what modern man needs – without interference of the Church and its authorities.

"Know thyself" is the inscription found on one of the walls in the temple of the oracle of Delphi. The god Apollo indicated that people should look for self-knowledge, gnosis, and this is what the great philosophers have always done.

In the Gospel of Thomas, Jesus says: "He who knows not himself knows nothing, but he who knows himself has acquired knowledge."

Gnosis makes us discover that we are immortal and that the physical body is not the most essential thing in our existence. Because of our greed, we lost sight of this essential theme. Spirituality brings the unique characteristics of people to the surface and enables us to experience a transformation within our consciousness.

Hopefully, people will not hesitate to opt for total surrender of the heart. Anyone who goes through this process of growth of consciousness, experiences it as a revelation. Revelation is a brilliant word: the essence is being revealed.

Contrary to the made-up story about Eden, the earthly Paradise, in which the man came first, the woman was seen as the first in the old cultures. Also, for the Cathars, woman was the goddess of life. The soul incarnates through a woman and she reveals. The man is there to assist her. That is why Jesus gave his wife, Mary Magdalene, the place she deserved.

The woman is the creative element within the androgyny of our human existence. In our time as well, the woman is important, because she, from her intuitive powers, stimulates the feminine part of the man.

The Gnostic writing *Pistis Sophia*, which resurfaced in the 18th century, tells us about Sophia, the female part of an androgynous emanation of Light, who took creative action. She formed a creature called Demiurge (half work). Because this creature originated outside the masculine part of the emanation, it was incomplete and not connected to the Light. Therefore, it disappeared into the chaos.

There, the Demiurge created matter and material man and thus he became the creator of heaven and earth. By the Love of the All, Sophia was given the chance to add *pneuma* (the Light) to people. This is why we are forever connected to the all-embracing Light, which Jesus referred to as *his Father*.

Life is a process of growth and development, of self-reflection and, in this process, we keep finding the answers to all kinds of questions and keep asking ourselves whether certain elements are still in accordance with our true Self.

The meaning of our lives is to rediscover ourselves, to relearn our lessons based on the experiences life provides us, and aside from that it is important that we face our positive and negative aspects by way of self-reflection.

Pain and sorrow are elements in our karmic life that help us grow. It is a good thing that we encounter all kinds of problems in our lives, because this enables us to learn and grow wiser. Problems are there to be solved and left behind. Many people have problems with letting go. Gnosticism teaches us that everyone is responsible for his own personal life. As long as people get stuck in their own problems, do not cut the knots, do not make decisions and can't let go, everything remains as it is, and things continue to repeat themselves, until we finally wake up.

Life means to be there in Love and Light, for our fellow beings, helping where we can and supporting people when they are lonely. Making contact, carrying a bag filled with joy and love. These rules of life are all very clear, and they were at the basis of the social and communal life of the Cathars. They had a just and harmonious society, which grew to be the most prosperous community in Europe.

During one of my journeys through the south of France, a Frenchman told me that the *Bon Hommes* (good people), as the Cathars were called, had the habit of saying, *au revoir* (so long) to their dying loved ones.

We often say "so long" to somebody, because we want to be polite, or we say it out of habit, when often we do not have the intention of coming back. Nevertheless, it is special to say this to a dying person. The deeper meaning was explained as follows: the phrase "au revoir" expressed the longing to see the soul of the dying person again in another life.

Some years ago, I assisted a man during his illness. He was terminal and said to me: "So long!" I loved it! This was a person who was aware of the fact that we will meet each other once again.

Instantly, I remembered the words of the Frenchman I had met. Their meaning does not become clear until we look at it more profoundly.

We need to look in a more refined way at our emotional and spiritual experiences. Our approach should be versatile, perceptive and holistic. Have we already forgotten what great philosophers like Erasmus, Einstein and Jung have taught us?

It would be better if all of us recognized that everything depends on love, peace and mutual solidarity. Our world would be a totally different place! It should start with the governments which represent the peoples, but in order to do this they should let go of their arrogance and their focus on the ego. It's all about equality and fraternity. Governments should serve the people and not the other way around, as is mostly the case presently. Let's stop eroding society by enlarging the gap between the rich and the poor.

After all, Christianity teaches us that man has been placed on this earth as a steward. The Church has never practiced this, despite the fact that they were the ones to spread the dogma. Mankind has received the earth to use, and revere as we would our mother and father, not to abuse it.

Gnosis confronts us with standards and values we are all familiar with, but which have fallen into the background. For Gnostics, it was of the utmost importance that all people are ethereally connected and evolve together, without necessarily being aware of it. According to their view, evolution happens outside the human field of perception and everything is so intricately interwoven that an encounter or even a smile have their effect on human karma.

They felt that "greatness" was expressed in a person's attitude to life, for instance by giving up an aspect of oneself in the interest of the other. Are you prepared to accept and respect others the way they are? Gnosticism teaches us that nobody is perfect, that everything belongs to everyone and that nobody can afford to place himself above someone else. Gnostics highlighted the fact that we are cosmically connected to one another, because we are all part of one big energy of life.

According to the Cathars, this energy of life is all around us. Nowadays, we call it the aura. The Cathars had no trouble accepting death – they chose the pyre above a forced conversion to Catholicism. They realized that death is no more than letting go of the physical body, and that we live on in the great universe. They knew there are three cosmic dimensions: the spirit, the soul and the body. These three dimensions together make up human existence. The body is our earthly vehicle. The soul or astral body is the vehicle in which we continue after death. The spirit is our entity, or who we truly are, and that is a part of the all-embracing primordial Principle of Life – the Light.

Most remarkable is the energetic connection between mankind and the cosmos. By way of our energy body, we are connected to other cosmic fields, but science totally ignores this. The Gnostics called it *Pleroma*, the Fullness of the original Emptiness. It forms itself within our brain and from there it gets divided into receiving and sending. This is of the utmost importance, because it is the way to get in touch with other human beings. The ether is constantly filled with all kinds of information, which we can receive. Our spirit has unlimited power. After all, we are connected to the collective unconscious, as noted in the writings of Carl Gustav Jung. In my view, he was not a "thinker," but got his inspiration from a deep wisdom we could call soul-knowledge. Jung and Einstein were not scientists who just worked from cognitive knowledge; they were more inspired from their inner knowledge. The same goes for plenty of others, but they may not be aware of this and would probably not be open to this view. Fortunately, there are also those that are aware of it. Mankind wishes to break through a certain paradox in order to capture the *Nothing*, but we cannot fathom the greatness of the cosmos. To compensate, theological science has created a divine being of the Primordial Principle and expressed in a human form, the Creator, which is worshipped by the Churches as their God. They do not worship the All, the Father, but the Demiurge. The chaos and gloom in this world, that were created by the Demiurge, has been simple-mindedly explained by the Church: Blame the Devil (which they invented). They used ruthless force, manufactured history and dreamed up clever rhetorical illusions that seemed to give a firm foundation for their great castles in the sky.

By accepting the World of Light, we experience the birth of the insight that "the *Nothing* is the *All*." For the World of Light is in fact, the situation in which we find ourselves after our death. It is the situation to which we belong. Time, space and limitation are parts of the material world. These concepts have no existence in the World of Light, and the same goes for Good and Evil. Long ago, I was walking along the seashore and I realized I was the only one on the beach. Suddenly, I felt tiny and insignificant. At that moment I realized that man, compared to the cosmos, is less than a grain of sand. Silence welled up from inside and I knew I could approach the *Nothing* from this silence. I felt a deep respect inside myself come up. Then it became clear to me that life fluctuates. There is a time for rising, a time for descending, and it is important to keep the balance. When one component keeps tearing down the other, we have to rediscover that which was lost.

Suddenly, I remembered a theory of Einstein's, in which he states that an object which moves forward by the speed of light loses its mass and is transformed into energy. During this process time slows down, gravity loses its grip and the zero point is reached, after which, time and gravity disappear completely. There are people who, by way of their strength of mind, can transform themselves and reach the same point. This form of manifestation is also found with the historical person Jesus. Because of his development, he had control over the material as well as the immaterial side of life, but the people around him had problems understanding his conduct, because of their lower consciousness. Hence, people saw his actions as supernatural – fully in line with the invented image of God by the Roman Catholic Church.

Many apocryphal texts state that if we want the light within us to remain radiant, we should not look for the dark, for then we will always fail. In this case, I think of one of Jesus' statements in an apocryphal writing of his brother James: "Do not turn the Kingdom of Heaven into a desert inside yourselves. Do not be proud of the Light that enlightens you, but be proud of yourselves, as I am proud of you. I have placed myself under the flesh, in order for you to be saved."

This text strikes me as very special. In simpler language one could say: do not turn your life into a barren desert, and do not think you have made it when you become aware of the ins and outs of things. Be kind to yourself, as I am to you. I want to pass this on to you, so you can become aware of it.

Gnosticism teaches us that all is in a constant flow of change (*Panta rhei*). It has to be so, because otherwise we would stagnate and not be able to grow. Gnosis shows us what we are doing and how we interact with others. We have to guide our children in this. This is very important, because in our society we encounter more and more children with high sensitivity. They have trouble dealing with injustice, unfairness and authoritarian behavior, which does not hold them in consideration. This is a great responsibility for the parents and for the educational system.

Spiritual growth, as a process of increasing awareness, is very resilient and gives us a clear direction. It makes us stronger and lends us more self-confidence. We gain insight into how and why certain processes take place. This helps us in dealing with them. It helps us to see the relativity of problems, leads us to inner peace and a more intensely engaged way of living.

The following Gnostic-inspired text was written in 1927, by Max Ehrmann. It has been an inspiration to millions and I include it here for those who haven't yet heard the message:

DESIDERATA

Go placidly amid the noise and the haste, and remember what peace there may be in silence. As far as possible, without surrender, be on good terms with all persons. Speak your truth quietly and clearly; and listen to others, even the dull and the ignorant; they too have their story.

Avoid loud and aggressive persons; they are vexatious to the spirit. If you compare yourself with others, you may become vain or bitter, for always there will be greater and lesser persons than yourself. Enjoy your achievements as well as your plans.

Keep interested in your own career, however humble; it is a real possession in the changing fortunes of time. Exercise caution in your business affairs, for the world is full of trickery. But let this not blind you to what virtue there is; many persons strive for high ideals, and everywhere life is full of heroism.

Be yourself. Especially, do not feign affection. Neither be cynical about love; for in the face of all aridity and disenchantment, it is as perennial as the grass.

Take kindly the counsel of the years, gracefully surrendering the things of youth. Nurture strength of spirit to shield you in sudden misfortune. But do not distress yourself with dark imaginings. Many fears are born of fatigue and loneliness. Beyond a wholesome discipline, be gentle with yourself.

You are a child of the universe, no less than the trees and the stars; you have a right to be here. And whether or not it is clear to you, no doubt the universe is unfolding as it should.

Therefore be at peace with God, whatever you conceive Him to be, and whatever your labors and aspirations are in the noisy confusion of life, keep peace in your soul.

With all its sham, drudgery and broken dreams, it is still a beautiful world. Be cheerful. Strive to be happy.

The Secret of
Southeastern France

The secret of southeastern France starts in the Pyrenees, to the south of Carcassonne, in the Cathar region. In about 1890, Bérenger Saunière, the pastor of the mountain village Rennes-le-Château, made the find of his lifetime.

Some years ago, a friend drew my attention to a book about this secret. Since then I have been studying it, and the intriguing story kept its grip on me.

In order to understand the history of this region, we have to go back in time.

In the first chapter we covered the *Desposyni*, the royal descendants of Jesus, Mary Magdalene and their children, and James, the Joseph of Arimathea. They fled to the south of France.

The second chapter dealt with what happened to the Merovingians, and how the Albigensians (the Cathars) were exterminated by the Church. The Merovingians and the Cathars both came forth from the dynastic line of the *Desposyni*.

The Holy Grail

When you hear this phrase, you probably see an image of a dish or a cup, in accordance with the traditional stories. But are these stories real?

People generally assume that the Grail is somehow connected to Jesus. And it is! According to some traditions, it was the cup from which Jesus and his disciples drank during the Last Supper. Or, it was the cup in which Joseph of Arimathea caught the blood of Jesus as he hung from the cross. Sometimes it was both. However, we must ask ourselves whether the Grail was a cup at all.

All stories that circulate about this subject have their origin in the Grail romances that were written in the 11th, 12th, and 13th centuries. Those times, like most times, were particularly dangerous for a free-thinker. The

Inquisition was in full operation and people had to be very careful about exercising their mouths. The Roman Catholic Church was a theological dictatorship, and, in most practical terms, the Church was the State. One could not say things that directly contradicted official paradigms, as is our right in the secular democracies many of us have the privilege of living in today – thanks to the heroic struggles and sacrifices which culminated in the American Revolution of 1776.

To escape the censorship and terror exercised by the Church, people were very inventive and used several forms of art in spreading their messages. Painters made use of symbols and authors used coded language, to communicate their heresies in cryptic ways discernible by those who had occult knowledge.

Percival, knight of the Grail, by Wolfram von Eschenbach is the most well-known book about the Grail. The author based his novel on information from someone he refers to as Kyot de Provence. There are no other references to this Kyot, but researchers managed to identify him. His true name appears to be Guiot de Provins, a troubadour from Provence. He was a monk and a spokesman for the Knights Templar.

Von Eschenbach tells the following story: Percival is a prince who is unaware of the fact that his father, who has passed away, was a knight. As a young man he meets some knights by accident, who impress him mightily. This motivates him to search for King Arthur, the only one who can grant him knighthood. After a long journey with many adventures he finally reaches the Grail fortress of King Arthur, who then knights him. This novel is filled with symbolism we can recognize from the Gnostic teachings. Percival's search for the Grail can be seen as an awakening, a growth process of the soul.

Percival discovers that he is a direct descendant of the Grail family. Reading this story, it becomes clear that the knights were the protectors of the Grail and the Grail family. The authors of the Grail romances had to take great care and could only pass on their secret message in a symbolic way.

In the self-interest of the Roman Catholic Church, the facts about the Priest Kings and the Grail family had to be suppressed. After the 7th century, they systematically destroyed thousands of documents, and therefore, there is little or no detailed history known about certain periods. During one period, common people were even expressly forbidden from learning to read and write; only the clergy were allowed to do this.

Of course, there were always folk tales, which were passed on orally. But they evolved, changed over time, which is understandable.

As the Church propagandists busily replaced inconvenient truths with their own inventions, certain knowledge survived by being passed on beneath the surface in allegorical form. It stands to reason that the Roman Catholic Church classified the Grail romances as heresy.

But what is this *Grail*, shrouded in mystery through the ages, in fact? A few centuries after the Grail romances appeared, suddenly the word *holy* was connected to it. The term "Holy Grail" was used for the first time by the Englishman Sir Thomas Malory, who edited the French *Saint Grail* in the 15th century, in *Le Morte d'Arthur*.

"Grail" was derived from the French word *Sangraal*. We just used the word Saint Grail, but it was a slip of the tongue or a misspelling, which was quite normal for that time. "Sangraal" is derived from *Sang Real* – "Sang" means blood and "Real" has to do with the royal line – royal blood. It is like a word game. This is how coded language was used: concepts were hidden in a way that was only understandable to insiders.

The question arises, "How is this related to France?" After the crucifixion, the pregnant Mary Magdalene fled from Palestine with some family members. They traveled, by boat, to the south of France, where they were safe within the large Jewish population.The "holy royal blood" originated from Mary Magdalene – a bowl or cup became the symbol of her womb. She was the carrier of the offspring of Jesus, which was hidden in the coded word *Sangreal*.

Jesus' wife gave birth to three children: Sarah-Tamar, Jesus and Joseph. The Hebrew name Sarah means *princess*, another confirmation for the term "Sang Real" which was used.

LANGUEDOC

It was a surprise to discover that in 1059, the church in Rennes-le-Château was devoted to Mary Magdalene. To this day, she remains the patron saint of the village.

It becomes even more remarkable when we discover this is not unique to Rennes-le-Château. All over the Languedoc we see images of her and many old churches and chapels are named after her. Did the people in this region perhaps know more than others? After all, the Catholic Church did not canonize Mary Magdalene until 1969.

In France, many stories are told that claim Jesus was still living in the Languedoc when he was 49 years old. It is unknown at what age he died, and this makes one wonder about the old expression, "Living like God in France." Mary Magdalene died at the age of 60, in the year 63, in what is now called

Sainte Baume, near Aix-en-Provence. Her skull is displayed in the basilica of the abbey of Saint Maximin, incorporated in a statue made of gold. To this day there are many people who smell the scent of roses in this church, while no roses are present. The rose is a symbol connected to Mary Magdalene. The road that leads to the basilica is called *Le Roi Chemin*, the King's Road.

According to another legend, she is buried in the basilica of Sainte-Marie-Madeleine, which was built in 1295 by Charles II of Anjou.

The Jewish community created an important energetic and spiritual foundation in south-eastern France, and they made this region for centuries the wealthiest part of France and even far beyond. The whole area still emanates a great peace and harmony, despite the fact that the Roman Catholic Church had a very negative impact on the region's history.

In order to keep our eyes on the connections and to understand the whole story, I have to provide some background information. This piece of the puzzle is very important.

In 410, the Visigoths plundered the city of Rome. Previous to that, the Romans had stripped Jerusalem and robbed, among other things, the treasures from the Temple of Solomon. The Visigoths were nomads who travelled throughout Europe and took their plunder with them on their journeys. When they arrived in the south of France, their leader, Alaric II, decided to stay. He occupied the Pyrenees and founded his kingdom. His throne was in Rhedae, which was renamed Rennes-le-Château later on.

Alaric II gave orders to dig deep cellars, which could only be entered through caves. And there are many caves in this neighborhood. He hid, according to possibly exaggerated accounts, at least 10,000 tons of gold and silver in these cellars against the depredations of future enemies. The Merovingian sovereign Clovis formed an army at the end of the 5th century. He waged war against the Visigoths and chased them out of France. Alaric II had no way of taking the immense hoard of treasures with him on his flight, and so they remained in Rhedae. It is remarkable that these treasures, originally belonging to the Davidian dynasty, ended up in the south of France as well.

RENNES-LE-CHÂTEAU

The Catholic priest Bérenger Saunière, became the pastor of the insignificant Rennes-le- Château in 1885. He was a poor man and lived a simple life in the little mountain village for several years. After that his life changed completely, because he found something remarkable.

The last time the old parish church had been restored was in the 15th century, and it had fallen into a dilapidated state. Saunière managed to get his hands on some money to make the most necessary repairs. During this renovation, he found ancient parchments hidden in a hollow altar pillar. He had discovered something very threatening to the Vatican's version of history, and a campaign quickly began to destroy it, in order to make the secret of southeastern France disappear forever. Luckily, they were unsuccessful, because one of the documents describes the family tree of Jesus' descendants.

Saunière got permission from the Bishop of Carcassonne to take these documents to Saint Sulpice, the religious headquarters in Paris. There he came in contact with people who were no good company for an orthodox Catholic priest, especially in those days. Some of them were artists, who had very specific esoteric ideas and occupied themselves with occult (spiritual) matters. In Paris he also started a long-lasting and intimate friendship with Emma Calvé, the internationally renowned opera singer.

Saunière must have had a very charismatic personality, because he was also an intimate friend of the countess of Chambord, who was married to the French crown pretender.

What happened in Paris is unknown, and we also do not know what was said to him, but I have my own suspicions. I think Saunière found out that the Roman Catholic Church dogma, including celibacy, had no legitimate foundation whatsoever. Hence his close relations with Emma Calvé.

To the Vatican it was very important that Saunière remain silent. In exchange for agreeing to this, he received a rich reward. It is a remarkable fact that Saunière, once he was back in Rennes-le-Château, lived a totally different, luxurious life! This was made possible by a visit from Archduke John of Habsburg, a cousin of Emperor Franz Joseph of Austria. Together they went to a local bank and Saunière opened an account, in which the archduke deposited a large sum of money.

The previously impoverished pastor suddenly started spending money like a millionaire. There is no official record of how he came by this unlimited supply of wealth, and he did not wish to account for it. The villagers benefited greatly from his generosity; they were regularly treated to sumptuous banquets, he had a water-tower built, and funded a paved road from the foot of the mountain to the top, where the village was situated.

The pastor lived in great opulence. A tropical garden with an orangery was laid out, as well as a garden with tropical animals. He collected rare porcelains, picture-postcards and stamps. He was a real *bon-vivant* and imported wines, liquors and delicacies from all over the world.

Saunière also carried out a radical, lavish and thorough restoration of his church using only the best craftsmen in the region. He took his time: the renovation went on for eleven years and included a large statue and some paintings of Mary Magdalene, one of which was placed at the front of the altar.

The way in which Saunière renovated his church was remarkable. He employed all kinds of arcane symbols, in order to share the secret he had discovered in the parchments, without violating his deal with the Vatican. In this subtle way, he ridiculed the Roman Catholic Church and its dogmatic ideas. But this was not the only place he confirmed the true status of Mary Magdalene. In the garden, in front of the church, Saunière had a cave built with a statue of Mary Magdalene, which was stolen a hundred years ago and has never been seen since. He also built the "Tour de Magdala," an enormous gothic tower, in which he housed an impressive library. He ordered books from all over the world and employed a full-time bookbinder.

He built a large and stately home, "Villa Bethania," where his housekeeper lived and many guests were received. Saunière himself remained in the old parsonage next to it.

Because this strange story had almost become a part of my daily life, I wanted, finally, to taste the atmosphere of Rennes-le-Château instead of just reading about it. So, I decided to go there. It was a special and revelatory experience.

Before I entered Bérenger Saunière's church, I was first confronted with a Latin motto affixed over the entrance: *Terribilis est locus iste* (This is a terrible place). With this saying, Saunière referred to the corruption and wantonness within the Catholic institution.

I entered the church and right behind the door was a high statue. The lower part depicted a devil, *Rex Mundi*. This "ruler of the world" is on his knees and forms a circle with his thumb and index finger: the Gnostic sign that "All is one." With the same hand he has pushed up his cape, so a knee and thigh are exposed.

I can't imagine anyone entering the church without noticing this alarming monstrosity. Saunière turned this "Rex Mundi," the king and ruler of the world, who is revered by Christians as God, into the symbol of this churchly institute. The Church has identified itself with this God and this shows clearly that, underneath the shallow cover of so-called holiness, only the material is revered. On his neck this devil carries a large font of holy water with four angels above it. These are symbols that have intoxicated humanity for ages. The dove, symbol of the Holy Spirit, completes the image. I recognized the elements: earth, water and fire.

Suddenly I became emotional, while looking at this huge statue. Tears rolled down my cheeks. I did not understand! I was even more amazed when, a moment later, I heard a clear voice saying: "Tell the world what you have seen!"

I was taken by surprise and looked at my wife and children, but they were simply walking around and viewing the church like the other visitors. It was clear to me that this was something only I had heard! My family members are used to the fact that I sometimes am transported outside the reality of here and now, but then at a certain moment, they noticed that I was not quite myself and kept an eye on me.

A moment later I heard the same voice again, repeating the same sentence and I asked: "Who are you?" The answer was: *I am Saunière. I discovered the lie and revealed everything in this church. Look closely at everything you see and I will make it clear to you. Tell the world that Jesus was not the Son of God, but a highly developed spirit. Rome turned it into a lie. When I was living on earth I had to remain silent, but I want you to speak for me now. Write everything down and I will enlighten you.*

Never did I have an experience that was as overwhelming as what happened to me that day. I was enjoying a vacation with my family and only wished to look around and see things and explore, but this… no, I had not expected this! It just overwhelmed me. It was such an intense experience; I had never encountered anything like it. Because I still felt very emotional and slightly dazed, I took a seat in the back of the church.

During the next days, I visited the church again, twice, and took my time looking at everything. I also took photographs.

There are many large statues and an enormous fresco. The decorations are incongruously extravagant – after all, it is only a small church. But they certainly capture the attention of the visitor, and that was Saunière's point. You can't get around it. There is no other choice but to see this!

I was quickly drawn to certain objects and many things were made clear to me.

At the bottom of the statue of Mary Magdalene I found this text: *Regnum mundi et omnem ornatum soeculi contempsi, propter anorem domini mei Jesu Christi, quem vidi, quem amavi, in quem cremini, quem dilexi.* This means: "I despised the kingdom of this world and its temporary adornments, by my love for my King Jesus Christ, whom I saw, whom I loved, in whom I believed and who I adored."

This is not a text from the Bible, it was written by John Tauler (1300-1361). Here is clearly the Cathar influence.

The fact that Saunière gave Mary Magdalene a central place in his church, emphasized how important she was in Jesus' life. The pastor had also, when he began the renovations, placed the statue of Mary, Jesus' mother, outside in the garden. This clearly shows how he felt about the adoration of Mary.

In the front of the church, he placed two life-sized statues. Joseph on one side and Mary on the other. They have no aureole, but both of them have a crown above their heads and they wear beautiful clothes. Saunière wanted to imply that Joseph and Mary were of royal descent. Each of them carries a child on the arm, meaning that they were a mother and father and had several children in a natural way. The children look related but are different individuals.

The baptism of Jesus by John the Baptist is also made fun of. The Bible speaks of John living in poverty, but Saunière had him portrayed in lavish Roman attire, with Jesus kneeling at his feet. By this he meant to say that Jesus was made subservient to the power of Rome.

In the same way, I discovered many messages in this "House of God," in which Saunière exposed the extant Roman Catholic dogma. He presented his views in an elliptical way, but when we look at the symbolism in detail, our eyes are opened.

Saunière also mocked the arrogance of the Christian Church. Normally we find the inscription IHS in churches, initials that refer to Jesus. But Saunière replaced them with his own initials: BS. They are found in several places, sometimes covering large parts of the walls! By this he meant to show that it was his building, his pulpit, and no longer a house of prayer belonging to the Church.

His initials are also used in combination with several ornaments, in which the French lily is prominent. The *fleur-de-lis* is the symbol of Mary Magdalene's offspring and, later on, the French royal dynasty.

Let's now look at the passion of Christ, the story of his suffering, as depicted in the 14 Stations of the Cross. Even they were given a modern character. Saunière included all kinds of unexpected details, which changes the general atmosphere. For example, in each station Jesus is wearing a royal dress, except for the last few, in which he is partially naked. In station number 4 he holds the hand of Mary Magdalene, who is accompanied by a little girl.

Saunière shows us how the Church took events out of context. He insisted on incorporating these signs, to help people discover the secret, by following unconventional patterns. The crucifixion is supposed to have taken place during the day, but, in station 14, Saunière exposes the lie of Golgotha with a full moon shining overhead.

Station 8 takes us to Scotland: a small child is wrapped in a Scottish tartan. Saunière is referring to the Stuart dynasty, which supposedly descends from the offspring of James, Jesus' brother.

All statues in the church wear royal robes. Saunière seems to have wanted to stress that. He wanted, before all, to display the riches of the soul, in order to show that the material side is insignificant. He makes a clear point of this with Saint Germaine. This female shepherd looks like a wealthy young woman. This tells us that the woman had a rich inner life, because she was connected to every living being.

In the Stations of the Cross and frescos, the church of Rennes-le-Château and the "Tour de Magdala" are visible on the background. This was Saunière's way of stressing how important the south of France had been in the life of Mary Magdalene and the blood line of Jesus.

We can conclude that the Roman Catholic Church is, on all fronts, founded on deceit. In his church, Saunière disclosed the truth, by way of provocative images.

He expressed very firmly that God is not a creature living far away in heaven, but that the Divine takes shape in yourself.

Bérenger Saunière had two good friends named Henri Boudet, Pastor of Rennes-les-Bains, and Antoine Gélis, Pastor in Coustaussa. They were completely different personalities, but nevertheless, this triumvirate was a closed circuit, fully aware of the secrets of the region. Boudet knew his surroundings so well that no cavern or cave was unfamiliar to him; Gélis was a progressive man, who lived from the heart and did not follow regulations.

These three men shared many inner experiences and I can well imagine that Saunière, at a certain time, told his secret to his friends.

The Church had trouble dealing with these three obstinate pastors. It was aware of the bonds between the three men and tried to uncover their secrets. At the dawn of the 20th century, the influence and intrigues of the Roman Catholic Church were still extensive. They shunned no method, whatever it took, to make sure their mythical dogma remained unaffected.

There was a sudden rupture in the trio when Gélis was slain in 1897. It was such a brutal murder, that it is hard to believe none of the neighbors heard any noise. The inside of the parsonage was entirely destroyed, and Gelis' body was so horribly mutilated that it was hard to identify him when he was found.

In that same year the pact fell apart completely, because after Gélis' death there was a split in the friendship between Boudet and Saunière, which was not healed until much later.

It is quite remarkable that all three pastors received a group of mysterious visitors shortly before their deaths. These men belonged to a fundamentalist faction, known within the Catholic Church as the "radical executioners of a movement," from which "Opus Dei" emanated in 1928.

Many very strange things have happened and have been discovered in Rennes-le-Château and its surroundings. Most of them cannot be explained.

Boudet and Saunière both died, in 1915 and 1917 respectively, under mysterious circumstances. Saunière died from a sudden stroke, but his death is shrouded in mystery and many questions remained unanswered.

When his last will was read, it became clear that Saunière was broke. He had probably, quite some time before his death, bequeathed his property to Marie, his loyal housekeeper. From the beginning she had been informed of what was going on.

Until 1946, Marie lived in Villa Bethania and led a very comfortable life. Everything changed when, following the Second World War, a new coin was introduced. People could only exchange their old francs for new ones if they could prove where the money came from. Under no conditions did Marie wish to disclose this secret. Villagers saw her burning big piles of old bank notes in the villa garden. During her seven remaining years, Marie led a sober life, getting by on the proceeds from the sale of the house. Marie did promise the couple who had bought Villa Bethania that before her death, she would reveal a secret that would make them rich and powerful. Alas, after suddenly suffering a stroke, she was paralyzed and lost the power of speech. Not long after this she died.

In this way, both Saunière and Marie took the secret with them to their graves.

Fortunately, the three village pastors left several clues which enabled researchers to deduce and conclude all kinds of things. Nevertheless, in southeastern France, there is still plenty to research and discover.

I am firmly convinced that the treasures from the Temple of Solomon, which the Visigoths hid underground, are still there. The same goes for the many precious items belonging to the Knights Templar, which also have never been found. The Knights Templar guarded another, more immaterial treasure: the dynasty of King David, which survived in the offspring of Jesus. This history remained hidden for centuries, but was fortunately rediscovered and made public in a cryptic and round-about way by Bérenger Saunière.

Epilogue

The religious life we are now familiar with in our Western society has been constantly elaborated on since it was invented during the early years of our Christian-era calendar.

Our real evolution is not based on theoretical and ideological thinking. It is a process that is based on a deeper emotional layer anchored within us. The essential core is what our inner voice tells us and how we cope with it. Unfortunately, not enough progress has been made regarding this, because most people do not take the time to listen. So, the old propaganda stubbornly remains in the mental superstructure of our world culture. We still cling to negative memes from the millennium-and-a-half in which the Church took advantage of illiteracy and social chaos in order to indoctrinate the people and to intimidate, persecute and murder anyone with a mind of their own.

On a positive note, the Church is no longer the frightening power it once was; otherwise, my life would be in danger as I write this sentence. *Gratia, vox populi.*

With this book, I have tried to show how the Christian churches (especially the Roman Catholic Church) came into being, how they made history and how they invented their own truth.

Today, more and more people are becoming aware that what we were taught during our religious education is not in accordance with the truth. There is no use in disguising and obscuring this deceit. We need to deal with it in all honesty and transparency.

Commonly, people's attitude towards the sovereigns of the Church testifies to a subservient pliability. I sometimes wonder: *Why?* Should we really keep looking at this institute through rose-colored glasses? Is it necessary to keep putting the Church on a pedestal? Should we keep surrounding this religion with an aura of holiness? No: the time has come to break up these harmful spirals.

The truth has been obscured by veils of deception for centuries. I would like to invite the churches to recognize this fact and to deal with the new situation in an adult manner. My motto for them is as follows:

Do not turn the Heavenly Kingdom inside you into a desert! Stop worshipping a God that does not exist, and accept the fact that God is the cosmic force in everything!

Spiritual awareness is experiencing an explosive growth and has become an irreversible process. It is useless to close our eyes to this new development. Spirituality gives us insight and transforms our way of thinking.

When we look at history in this way, it becomes easier to let go of *yesterday* and to live in the *present* – this applies to the perpetrator as well as the victim. In the end everybody has fallen victim to the system…

I too have fallen victim to this churchly institution. The trauma, which I was formerly not aware of, presented itself to me like a knot of interwoven ropes, which was almost impossible to disentangle. I could only start to disentangle it once the nature of the trauma I carried became clear to me.

Until that moment years went by filled with pain, misery and sadness. I struggled with myself and had no clue as to what I was struggling against. I compensated, shouted myself down and overruled everyone and everything around me. It made me hurt people and I acquired the stigma of being a difficult man, which is the reason people who were very dear to me disappeared from my life. In my natural pattern of behavior, I sought after formulas without really knowing for what I was searching – until I was taken by surprise by muscular rheumatism, which made my life fall to pieces. Indirectly, I met a man who could have been my brother and who saw through me. Never before did I cry like I did in that moment.

After I had done some more work on the manuscript that preceded this book, I looked in the mirror and saw the true nature of my trauma. My disease purified me and helped me process everything.

I overcame all of this and in retrospect I can say that, not only have I become a different person, I have become the man I always wanted to be, from my loving and kind-hearted side.

In Love and Light,
Maurits Prins

BIBLIOGRAPHY

Alders, Hanny: *In het spoor van de Katharen,* (In the wake of the Cathars), Published by Conserve, 1999, the Netherlands (not available in English).

Andrews, Richard & Schellenberger, Paul: *The Tomb of God*, Published by Pactolus, London, 1996.

Baigent, Michael; Leigh, Richard & Lincoln Henry: *The Holy Blood and the Holy Grail*, Published by Jonathan Cape, London, 1982.

Churton, Tobias: *The Gnostics*, Published by George Weidenfield & Nicolson, London, 1987.

Dutch Bible Society: 1997 edition of the Bible – New Testament.

Feather, Robert: *The Copper Scroll Decoded*, Published by Thorsons, London, 1999.

Gardner, Sir Laurence: Bloodline of the Holy Grail, Published by Element Books, Shaftesbury, Dorset, 1996

Gardner Sir Laurence: *The Magdalene Legacy, the Jesus and Mary Bloodline Conspiracy*, Published by Element / Harper Collins Publishers, London, 2005.

Jung, Carl Gustav: *Conscious and Unconscious*, Published by Lemniscaat, 1997, the Netherlands – as a part of the Collected Works by Carl Gustav Jung;published by Routledge & Kegan Paul, London and by Princeton University Press, Princeton, U.S.A.

Mathieu-Rosay, Jean: *La Véritable Histoire des Papes* (The true Story of the Popes), Published by Grancher, Paris, 1991.

Moerland, Bram: *Katharen en de Val van Montségur* (Cathars and the downfall of Montségur), Published by Mirananda, 1992, the Netherlands (not available in English).

Quispel, Gilles: *Valentinus de Gnosticus en zijn Evangelie der Waarheid* (Valentine, the Gnostic and his Gospel of the Truth), Published by In de Pelikaan, 2003, the Netherlands (not available in English).

4

Slavenburg, Jacob & Glaudemans, Willem: *Nag Hammadi Geschriften Part I & II* (containing the Gospels of Mary Magdalene, Thomas and Philip), Published by Ankh-Hermes, 1995, the Netherlands.

Meyer, Marvin & Robinson, James: *The Nag Hammadi Scriptures*, Published by Harper Collins Publishers, 2009.

Slavenburg, Jacob: Valsheid in *Geschrifte* (Forgery of Documents) Published by Walburg Pers, 1997, the Netherlands (not available in English).

Slavenburg, Jacob: *Maria Magdalena en haar Evangelie* (Mary Magdalene and her Gospel), Published by Ankh-Hermes, 2002, the Netherlands (not available in English).

Slavenburg, Jacob: *De vrouw die Jezus lief had* (The woman Jesus loved), Published by Walburg Pers, the Netherlands (not available in English).

Slavenburg, Jacob: *Onbekende Woorden van Jezus* (Unknown Words of Jesus), Published by Altamira, the Netherlands (not available in English).

Slavenburg, Jacob: *Gnosis*, Published by Ankh-Hermes, the Netherlands (not available in English).

Slavenburg, Jacob: *De mislukte Man* (The failed man), Published by Alpha, the Netherlands (not available in English).

Spalding, Baird: *Life and Teachings of the Masters of the Far East* Published by The Vorss & Co, USA.

Stichting, Teleac: *De Zoon van God* (The Son of God) video tape, 2003-2004, the Netherlands (not available in English).

Unknown: *Die Bibel ist gefälscht – Hiëronymus, der kirchliche Bibelfälscher* (The Bible has been falsified - Jerome, the churchly Bible falsifier), Published by Verlag DAS Wort, Germany / Dutch publication in 2006.

Van Schaik, John: *Het beeld van Jezus Christus door de Eeuwen heen* (The Image of Jesus Christ throughout the Centuries), Published by Christofoor, 2002, the Netherlands (not available in English).

Von Eschenbach, Wolfram: *Percival, Knight of the Grail*, Published by Vrij Geestesleven, Zeist, 1977, the Netherlands and by Penguin Classics, London, 1980.

Yallop, David: *In God's Name*, Published by Jonathan Cape, London, 1984